Global Warming

Other titles in the Issues in Focus *series:*

Issues in Focus

Global Warming
Understanding the Debate

Kenneth Green

Enslow Publishers, Inc.

40 Industrial Road PO Box 38
Box 398 Aldershot
Berkeley Heights, NJ 07922 Hants GU12 6BP
USA UK

http://www.enslow.com

The author wishes to acknowledge the patient and loving encouragement of his wife, Patricia Green, without whose help this book would not have been finished.

Library of Congress Cataloging-in-Publication Data

Green, Kenneth Philip, 1961-
    Global warming : understanding the debate / Kenneth Green.
        v. cm. — (Issues in focus)
    Includes bibliographical references and index.
    Contents: The debate over global warming — What is this theory of global warming? — Hard evidence of global warming — Circumstantial evidence of global warming — The primary suspects: greenhouse gases — Questionable characters — So whodunnit? — What can be done?
    ISBN 0-7660-1691-9
    1. Global warming—Juvenile literature. [1. Global warming.]
I. Title. II. Issues in focus (Hillside, N.J.)
QC981.8.G56 G725   2002
363.738'74—dc211
                                2002000275

Printed in the United States of America

10 9 8 7 6 5 4 3 2 1

To Our Readers:
We have done our best to make sure all Internet addresses in this book were active and appropriate when we went to press. However, the author and the publisher have no control over and assume no liability for the material available on those Internet sites or on other Web sites they may link to. Any comments or suggestions can be sent by e-mail to comments@enslow.com or to the address on the back cover.

Illustration Credits: All photos are from Corel Corporation, except for the following: Digital imagery copyright 1999 PhotoDisc, Inc., pp. 77, 85; EyeWire Images, p. 104; Jose Lopez, Jr.,/National Science Foundation, p. 90; National Science Foundation, p. 57; Painet Stock Photos, p. 62.

Cover Illustration: Digital imagery copyright 1999 PhotoDisc, Inc.

17376

Contents

The Debate Over Global Warming

Global warming. An idea that few people had heard of twenty years ago now fills the pages of newspapers, magazines, and science journals every day. If the weather turns hot, if a glacier seems to be melting, if spring comes a few days early one year, or if a drought seems a little longer than normal, the newspapers, radio, and television will explode with global warming stories. And the headlines are rarely positive. Stories about increases in flooding, drought, forest fires, hurricanes, and disease are all linked to claims that the earth is heating up and that humanity is causing a large part of that change.

At research universities, private research institutions, and government research centers, studies of weather, and of longer-term weather patterns called *climate*, have never been more intense. Every year, billions of dollars are spent on global warming research. In the year 1999, President Bill Clinton proposed spending over $4.5 billion to study or prevent global warming.[1] Science writers study the scientific literature and interview scientists looking for information to use in newspaper, television, and radio news stories.

The desire to study and talk about global warming—and its effects on climate—has become the central focus of thousands of scientists, engineers, economists, politicians, business leaders, students, and others.

Why all the sudden interest? Though the human desire to understand the climate is a long one, the current focus on climate was really triggered by one particularly powerful season.

The Wacky Weather of 1988

In 1988, the weather broke out of its previous normal patterns, starting with an unusually hot spring, moving through a blistering summer, and ending with a strangely hot autumn. Some scientists, long worried that human action could change the earth's climate, felt that the weather of 1988 was so unusual that it just could not be natural. They suggested that the weather of 1988 was the "smoking gun" that conclusively tied human activity to the warming of the earth's surface. Ever since that summer, the world has been on a "climate watch," with thousands of scientists around the world looking for signs that human activities are causing changes in the earth's climate.

Though the United States (and the rest of the world) had seen heat waves before, 1988 was a big one by anyone's standards. May is normally a month when the pleasant temperatures of spring inspire people to pack picnic baskets, admire wildflowers, and go

During the wacky summer of 1988, New York (shown above) was not the only city with blistering temperatures; the weather was unusually warm in many parts of the world.

on family outings. But that was not the case in 1988. By May of 1988, things were already abnormally warm in many parts of the United States. Record high temperatures were recorded in thirteen cities across the United States. Mild spring temperatures had come to an early end, and the heat of summer was coming on with a vengeance.

But a sweltering month of May was only the beginning of 1988's weather woes. By June, another sixty-nine American cities broiled under record high temperatures. Energy use soared as people sought escape from the heat in air-conditioned buildings. By July, another thirty-seven American cities found themselves cooking, and there was more to come. In San Francisco, the temperature hit 103°F on July 13, setting a new record in the city's history.[2] Thirty-one more cities reached record high temperatures by August. In Los Angeles, the temperature hit 110°F in September, causing many people to turn up their air conditioners, sending the demand for electricity skyrocketing. The demand was so high that the city's electrical system could not keep up: Four hundred electrical transformers burned out in a single day.[3] In North Carolina, the heat was so bad during one week in August that it killed more than 166,000 chickens and 15,000 turkeys.[4]

Excessive heat was not the only unusual feature of 1988's weather patterns. It was also an unusually dry year. In fact, the inland parts of the United States had not seen such hot and dry weather for fifty years. But coastal areas felt the heat also, and the drought was still worse in the southeastern United

States. Some parts of the country had not seen such dry weather for one hundred years. In Michigan that summer, there was not only a drought, there were also thirty-nine days when it was 90°F or higher, breaking a record set during the "great dustbowl" days of 1934.[5] The dryness and heat in the summer of 1988 were devastating to farmers. Without rain, crops did not grow as well. Crops produced 30 to 40 percent less food than usual across the nation. The parched soil, normally a fertile planting ground, had turned inhospitable. Even where crops grew, they were stunted. As areas were starved of rainfall, water levels fell in lakes and rivers. Nightly news programs showed pictures of boats stuck in the mud of a shrunken Mississippi River. Cameras panned over vast expanses of parched and cracked fields and giant channels of sunbaked mud that had once been powerful rivers.

It got worse. Before the end of the summer, massive fires broke out in Yellowstone National Park, burning about 36 percent of the park, or nearly 1.2 million acres by August 1988.[6] That was the largest area of Yellowstone to burn in nearly one hundred years. By comparison, in the prior sixteen years, 235 small fires had only burned about 34,000 acres altogether. In mid-September, Hurricane Gilbert, an unusually powerful hurricane, caused massive damage in the Yucatán, a peninsula in southeast Mexico between the Caribbean Sea and the Gulf of Mexico. Mexico, Texas, and other parts of the world suffered too. In some places there were severe floods, as weather patterns dropped too much water on some parts of the world, while the United States was desperately parched. Almost 80 percent of Bangladesh (a very poor country in South Asia) was hit by a flood that summer, the fifth severe flood to hit them in eight years. And more than three thousand people died in India from a heat wave of historic proportions.[7]

When the worldwide temperature records were studied at the end of 1988, it turned out to have been the hottest year recorded in those areas since humans started keeping temperature measurements more than 120 years before. It was also the fifth year in a row that had hotter-than-average temperatures, making the 1980s the warmest decade in 127 years.

Yellowstone National Park, home to many types of plants and animals, was the site of terrible forest fires during the summer of 1988. Over a third of the park land was burned.

Looking for Explanations

The heat, floods, droughts, and fires of 1988 were like the starter's pistol shot at a track meet, setting off a global race for answers. Why was it so hot? What was causing the droughts? What was causing the floods? What was causing the fires? Possible suspects were quick to emerge.

On only the second day of summer, when temperatures in Washington, D.C., had already reached a blistering 101°F, James Hansen, director of NASA's Goddard Institute of Space Studies, was invited to testify before the U.S. Senate committee on Energy and Natural Resources. Hansen said, "My principal conclusions are; number one, the earth is presently warmer than at any time in the history of instrumental measurements. Number two, the greenhouse effect is probably the principal cause of the current global warmth. Number three, our computer climate simulations suggest that the greenhouse effect is already large enough to affect the probability of extreme events such as summer heat waves."[8]

In linking the warming of 1988 to an increase in the greenhouse effect, Hansen was pointing the finger of blame squarely at humanity. James Hansen was not the first person to link human actions to global weather patterns by any means. But his testimony, coming at the start of 1988's unusual weather, made him seem like a prophet of global doom and launched a massive global effort to learn about global warming.

Since 1988, human understanding of global

warming and the earth's climate have improved in many ways. Technology has improved our ability to measure how the climate changes day by day. And equally important, advances in computer science have improved our ability to explore how the greenhouse effect works. Scientists have long known that certain gases in the air (called *greenhouse gases*) trap some of the energy from incoming sunlight, keeping the surface of the earth warmer than it would be without those gases. This is called the *greenhouse effect*, and the extra heat trapping is called *global warming*. Scientists have also seen that human actions have changed the amount of greenhouse gases in the air, and many scientists think this may be causing more heat trapping at the surface of the earth. Finally, climate investigators are fairly certain that the average temperature near the surface of the earth has risen a bit in the last 120 years. But in other ways, uncertainty has only grown.

The Intergovernmental Panel on Climate Change

The biggest group of climate investigators in the world was formed shortly after James Hansen's historic testimony. Run by the United Nations, the Intergovernmental Panel on Climate Change, or IPCC, brings together scientists and other climate researchers from around the world to study and write about global warming and climate change. Every five years, the IPCC publishes a massive report that summarizes much of what is known or suspected about

In Washington, D.C., temperatures were over 100°F by the second day of summer in 1988.

climate change. The newest report, called the Third Assessment Report, is over three thousand pages long.[9]

In the Third Assessment Report, investigators weigh the evidence gathered to study global warming. Their conclusion is that the earth's atmosphere is not only getting warmer, but that human action has been causing the recently observed global warming. The IPCC also suggests that other types of climate change have already happened because of the extra heat. But IPCC researchers try to look ahead as well as back, and in the Third Assessment Report, the IPCC investigators predict that a warmer atmosphere will cause more weather like that of 1988. They say that a warmer world will have faster changing weather, with more droughts in some places and more floods in others. IPCC investigators also suggest that changes in the climate will affect animal and insect life as well, forcing some animals to move to cooler areas and causing some animals to become extinct altogether. Other animals, including some insect pests, according to the IPCC investigators, might have to move from their present habitat and shift into new areas, causing disruption among local animal and human populations that are not used to their presence.

But even in the reports of IPCC investigators, many careful statements of doubt surround those claims, raising as many questions as answers. And some climate investigators, both inside and outside the IPCC, dispute the validity of some or all of these predictions. These doubting investigators say that the scientific theories of global warming and climate change are still too immature to allow for really accurate climate forecasts. Sometimes called skeptics, these investigators point out that not enough is really known about the earth's past climate to know if recent weather is really abnormal or whether humanity's limited history of weather-watching only makes it look that way. They point out that scientific understanding of the possible causes of global warming and climate change keep shifting over time, with old suspected causes being dismissed and new suspected causes being discovered. And the skeptical investigators argue that not nearly enough is known about the way the earth works to predict what weather patterns might be like even in the near future, much less one hundred or one thousand years into the future, as the IPCC investigators propose to do.

Efforts to understand global warming and the effects that warming might have on the weather are more than just another attempt to answer obscure scientific questions about the weather. Human prosperity in many parts of the world, particularly developing countries, depends largely on the climate. Rainfall, drought, days of sunshine, days of frost, and the potential for severe weather all affect the functioning of human societies and the health of the natural systems they depend upon. Agriculture, tourism, transportation, energy use, and many other activities that define our cities and states are heavily influenced by the climate.

Important Questions

The quest to understand global warming is also different from most other scientific pursuits. While most scientific pursuits take place in laboratories and are worked on by people specializing in only one field of science, the global warming investigation is a fascinating detective story in which thousands of climate investigators from different scientific and even nonscientific specialties are trying to answer important questions about the planet we live on.

Some investigators are trying to figure out if the surface of the earth is warming up abnormally. If the earth is warming up abnormally, other investigators want to know if humans are to blame.

If humans are to blame, still more investigators want to figure out which human actions are causing the warming.

If it is warming, and if humans are to blame, still other researchers are trying to figure out how the earth's surface might react to such warming or changes in the atmosphere. Does the earth have natural mechanisms that would preserve the comfortable temperature range in which humans thrive, or could the whole climate system be pushed off balance and run out of control, to temperature levels that humans would find intolerable?

Finally, other investigators wonder what a warmer earth would be like to live in. Would sea levels be higher? If so, where would it rise and how high would it get? Would it rain more? Would hurricanes and other violent storms become more frequent?

Would all the ice melt at the North and South Poles? How would farming be affected? What about natural ecosystems like forests, deserts, and swamps?

And then, some investigators are asking what humanity ought to do if the earth is warming up and if especially harsh climate troubles are looming in the future.

Humanity has always been fascinated with the climate. In ancient times, human beings built many devices to track the change of the seasons. For example, Stonehenge is an ancient monument built

Stonehenge, built in England over three thousand years ago, is believed to have been used by ancient people as a type of observatory to study the position of the sun, the moon, and the stars.

in stages between 2800 and 1500 B.C. in the area now known as England. Based on the position of the sun, moon, and stars sighted over the various stones, Stonehenge could have been used to determine when the seasons were going to change. Such knowledge may have been used by primitive farmers to determine when to plant and when to hold religious ceremonies. Farmers were our earliest known climate watchers, always looking for telltale signs of impending rain or drought, frost or heat. But even before agriculture, humans had to deal with changing seasons, needing shelter from harsh weather, and having to plan ahead to insure the availability of food.

Since the earliest days of human existence, knowing what kind of weather was coming was vitally important for human survival. Thousands of years after the construction of Stonehenge, humanity is still trying to understand the way the world works and what the future holds in terms of nasty weather.

2

What Is This Theory of Global Warming?

Weather, as everyone knows, changes from day to day. Anyone who has made plans based on weather reports also knows that predicting the weather is very difficult. But over longer periods of time, weather becomes more predictable, forming distinct seasons that are similar year after year. Those long-term weather patterns are what people are talking about when they discuss the climate. Over the short term of decades or centuries, the climate seems to be pretty regular. Most years seem to have similar climate patterns to the year before, and those patterns seem to stay the same decade after decade. The new year starts with winter, slides into spring, then summer, and then fall. Some years have summers that are warmer than average or winters that are colder than average, but the winter is still nearly as cold as the year before and the summer nearly as warm.

Small changes from year to year are a natural part of the climate system. But within the regular parade of seasons, there are also long-term trends that are harder to spot. Rather than changing randomly, winters may be colder than average for several years in a row, or summers may be a bit hotter than average for more than one year at a time. Fall might be wetter for several years running, or spring might be dryer. And such long-term changes and trends are not always predictable. Evidence from studies of the past tells us that the earth's climate has made some very sharp and unexplained changes in the past.

Why the Variation?

The natural changeability (or variability) of the earth's climate flows from the nature of earth itself, a planet orbiting a sun, in a system with other planets. The earth's orbit, or the path it travels around the sun, is very complicated. One thing that makes the earth's orbit complicated is that the earth does not make a perfect circle around the sun. Rather, the earth swings around the sun on an oval, or elliptical, pathway. That means that sometimes, the earth is closer to the sun, and sometimes it is farther away. When it is farther away from the sun, the earth receives less energy from the sun than it does when the earth and sun are closer to each other. Another factor about earth's orbit that affects the climate is that the earth is tilted on its axis, the imaginary line that runs through the earth from the North Pole to the South Pole. That means that sometimes one part of the earth will lean in toward the sun, while the rest leans away. Still another complication is that the earth sometimes wobbles on its axis, exposing different parts of the earth to greater sunlight than at other times. And of course, the earth has a moon orbiting around it. The mass of the moon causes a gravitational pull on the earth, changing the patterns of water flow in the oceans and changing the patterns of air flow around the earth. Both the air and water flows on the earth's surface move heat around and cause changes in the local weather. On top of all that is a thick layer of unpredictability because of what scientists call "chaos." Chaos is the tendency of complex systems to have undetectable features that can cause sudden and unpredictable changes in their normal patterns of behavior.[1]

Because of all those factors that affect the earth's orbit, the planet's climate has always changed over time, putting the earth through many short- and long-term temperature cycles of warmth and cold. At various times in the past, ice ages have dominated the earth, covering huge swaths of the planet in a cloak of massive glaciers and freezing temperatures. At such times, the world was very much colder than it is today. The last major ice age began about 3 million years ago, and though there have been some short warm periods since then, that major ice age is just now ending. At other times, such as the late Cretaceous period 65 million years ago, our planet was a much warmer place, mostly covered in lush jungles and swamps, where dinosaurs such as *Tyrannosaurus rex* roamed the earth.

Of course, human beings were not around to take temperature readings in those dinosaur days. And, even when people did appear on the scene about 4 million years ago, they did not know how

The moon exerts a gravitational pull on the earth, affecting ocean tides and the flow of air around the earth.

to measure the temperature. That ability did not exist until Galileo developed a type of thermometer in A.D. 1593.

Still, despite the lack of early records, modern scientists investigating the climate have found very interesting ways of estimating what the earth's temperature was like long ago. By gathering a variety of evidence from tree rings and corals, and by taking temperatures from deep inside the earth, scientists have built an understanding of earth's temperature patterns that extend far back before humans were temperature takers.

The History of Climate

Figure 1 shows the history of earth's temperature far into the past, as nearly as investigators can puzzle it out from such indirect evidence. Some of this evidence from the distant past, and how investigators gather it, will be discussed later.

As you can see from the figure, the average temperature of the earth has changed dramatically throughout history. Today's temperatures, while warm, are not as warm as some previous periods. And back in the dino days of the Triassic and Jurassic periods, temperatures were quite warm by comparison with more recent times.

So with all this natural change and climate variation, why do people think that humans might be causing the global warming talked about in all the news headlines? Well, the earliest known references to the potential ability of human beings to cause

FIGURE 1: Earth's Surface Temperature Through History[2]

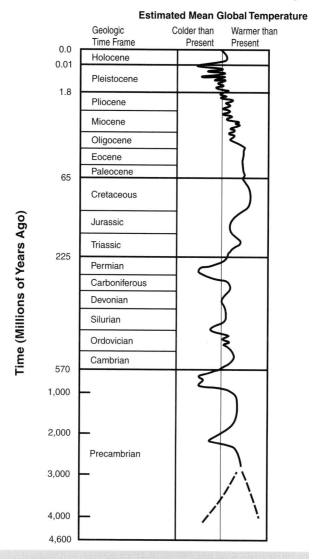

Note: The dotted line in the Precambrian period indicates that scientists are too uncertain about the climate beyond 3 million years ago to say whether it was warmer or cooler than it is now.

changes in their own climate came from a man named Theophrastus.[3]

Theophrastus was a student of Aristotle, the Greek "Father of Philosophy," and studied with him in the third century B.C. The observation that got Theophrastus into the science history books was not about global temperature but was about the way that swamps can change local temperatures. Theophrastus noted that when people drained the water from local swamps (now often called wetlands), the local temperature in the local area got colder. Theophrastus also noted that when people removed local forests, the local area became warmer. But in those days, there was little knowledge of how big the world was or how things worked at the level of the entire planet.

Much later in history, in the 1750s, David Hume, a philosopher from Scotland, speculated that the spread of farming had changed the climate of Europe. He noted that the removal of trees and draining of wetlands to allow planting of crops had changed the local climate in Europe. Hume speculated that America, with its rapidly growing agricultural activities, could experience similar change. Still closer to home, Thomas Jefferson, the author of America's Declaration of Independence, also believed that settlement in America would change weather patterns, but for the better. Jefferson believed that settlement in America would tame the harsh climate of the New World. But Jefferson thought that any changes that humanity made to the

The climate of our planet has varied over time. For instance, the earth was much warmer during the days of the dinosaurs.

climate would be beneficial and allow for a more comfortable existence.[4]

These early climate watchers, Theophrastus, Hume, and Jefferson, were mostly talking about *local* changes in the climate. These kinds of changes are well known in our scientific understanding of humanity's impacts on local weather patterns. Today's climate researchers, by contrast, focus first on changes that affect the whole planet and then try to understand how those global changes might cause local climate changes.

But today's climate investigators are also looking for answers to other questions. They do not only want to know if the climate is warming and how that might cause local changes. They also want to know why the climate is changing. They want to know if human activity has played a role in the warming that seems to have happened since the 1800s. Did humanity's conversion of forests into croplands have something to do with it? Was it humanity's increased use of fossil fuels? Could methane, a gas that is produced when growing rice, be part of the problem? Furthermore, today's climate researchers are not only looking backward, they also want to know how much human activity might change the global climate in the future. Will human activity have only a tiny impact on the earth's climate, or might it have a major impact? Today's climate investigators are looking for the effects that people can have on the earth at all levels, from local to global, through the way they change air that we breathe and the land upon which we live.

The Global Warming Theory

The main theory that climate investigators base their research on is the theory of global warming. The theory of global warming explains the way certain gases, called greenhouse gases, keep the earth's surface warmer than it would be if the air held less of those gases. Unlike previous studies of global warming that just tried to figure out how the earth's temperature was regulated, the modern theory of global warming focuses on humanity and its impacts. Scientists are struggling to understand not only how the climate works, but also how humanity's actions in changing the level of greenhouse gases in the air could be changing the average temperature of the earth's surface.

The theory of global warming has a long and distinguished history, but the most important elements of the theory stem from two very early observations. The first observation is that certain gases can change the way the earth's atmosphere, the layer of air surrounding the earth, retains heat. The second observation is that human beings do things that can change the levels of those gases in the atmosphere.

Fourier and Tyndall Investigate

In 1822, a man named Joseph Fourier investigated the first key observation that rests at the heart of the theory of global warming, which is that certain gases can affect the movement of heat. Fourier was better known as a mathematician, but he also investigated other scientific issues, and studying heat was a strong interest of his. Fourier was especially interested in the way that heat moves from one object to another through space, air, or solid matter. One of the many heat-related questions that Fourier sought to answer was why the air inside a greenhouse stays so much warmer than the air outside it. Earlier investigators had shown that while glass would let some kinds of heat energy such as sunlight pass through easily, it would stop other kinds of heat energy, such as the heat that you might feel coming from a rock that had been heated up during the daytime.[5]

But Fourier wanted to look beyond the glass and see if other forces were also changing the way heat was trapped in a greenhouse. And that led to Fourier's biggest contribution to the understanding of global warming—his theory that in addition to solid things like glass, transparent gases, of the sort found in earth's atmosphere, could also change the way the earth captures heat from the sun. Following the scientific method of making observations, then making predictions, and then doing experiments, Fourier demonstrated that his theory was correct. Fourier measured how glass plates would prevent the movement of certain types of heat, all by themselves. Then, using glass boxes filled with either a vacuum or regular air, Fourier measured how heat passed into and out of the boxes. He observed that both the glass and the gas inside were important to regulating the temperature on the inside of the box. From these observations, Fourier concluded that indeed, certain gases in the atmosphere were able to trap some of the incoming heat from the sun and hold it close to the earth's surface.

By modern standards, Fourier's experiments were fairly simple, but his discoveries were big enough to allow later investigators to give substance to the theory of global warming. Still, it was not until the middle of the nineteenth century that the first really convincing experiments were done to demonstrate the heat-trapping ability of atmospheric gases.

In the mid-1800s, an Irishman named John Tyndall took up where Fourier had left off. Tyndall, the son of a part-time shoemaker and constable, went on to study mathematics and science at universities in England, where he investigated the heat-trapping ability of a variety of gases, not just regular air.[6]

In 1859, Tyndall began a series of experiments that would expand greatly upon the ideas of Fourier. Rather than just testing plain air, Tyndall tested several gases, as well as water vapor, for their ability to trap heat. Tyndall showed that carbon dioxide, water vapor, nitrous oxide, and ozone (a gas made up of three atoms of oxygen bound together) could strongly affect the way that heat was trapped in the atmosphere.[7] Tyndall went on to show how some of these transparent gases could trap heat more strongly than others, and he even looked at the way that smog and soot could scatter light and affect the retention of heat in the atmosphere. That phenomenon would eventually bear his name and be called the Tyndall Effect. Tyndall's findings were quite exciting in his time, because he did his research in an age when people were not used to the idea that invisible things (like water vapor) could have very strong effects on the environment. Now that people are used to that idea, it does not seem so revolutionary. But back then, Tyndall was breaking new ground.

Arrhenius Theorizes

The theory of global warming was fully formed in 1895, when Swedish scientist Svante Arrhenius suggested that carbon dioxide could function as a greenhouse gas not only to boost the temperature of greenhouses, but also to regulate the surface temperature of the entire planet. Arrhenius also took the next logical step in thinking about the climate, noting that humanity's ability to change carbon dioxide concentrations could lead to changes in the climate we experience year after year. Arrhenius, who was born just when John Tyndall started studying the heat-trapping nature of gases, speculated that this global warming would be beneficial, just as plants grow better in a warm greenhouse than they do outside in colder areas.[8]

Besides putting the finishing touches on the basic

Human activities such as farming are thought to play a role in changes in the earth's climate. Shown is a sorghum field in rural Africa.

theory of human-caused, or *anthropogenic*, global warming, Arrhenius was the first climate investigator to put some hard numbers to the theoretical relationship between carbon dioxide and the earth's temperature. And despite one hundred years of additional climate investigation, Arrhenius's predictions are still close to current estimates of the temperature-changing impacts of increasing the level of carbon dioxide in earth's atmosphere.

New Discoveries

Until recently, all this study of global warming was highly theoretical. The effect could be predicted but had never really been observed. Some global warming researchers (such as NASA's James Hansen) think that has changed, however, and that the climate has started to change directly because of human activity. It was during the industrial revolution, which began around 1850, that human use of fossil fuels increased dramatically and human impacts on the distribution of forests, prairies, and other ecosystems became widespread. Hansen suggests that changing greenhouse gas levels will also lead to changes in other weather events such as rainfall and snowfall. Those changes, in turn, could affect whether rivers dry up and whether glaciers grow or shrink. Thus, some climate investigators suggest, humanity's alteration of atmospheric concentrations of greenhouse gases could explain the unusual warmth of the last fifty years or so.

Some researchers suggest that humanity's

production of greenhouse gases has already caused warming of the overall environment. They think that these temperature changes are already causing changes in natural cycles such as air currents, ocean currents, evaporation, and plant growth. More changes are predicted as time goes on, particularly in the rainfall and evaporation cycles of the earth. Some researchers think that global warming will cause a rise in the earth's sea level due to the heating of the oceans (which makes them expand) and the melting of sea ice, ice sheets, or polar ice caps. Other researchers think that stronger activity in the earth's cycle of rainfall and evaporation could lead to floods in some areas or droughts in other areas. Some fear that rising sea levels could swamp some coastal areas or low-lying islands. Furthermore, when sea levels get higher, the salty ocean water can change freshwater coastal zones to salty or even make underground water supplies too salty to drink.

Going even farther down the chain of cause and effect, some climate investigators have predicted a series of thirdhand impacts that might occur if the climate warms and climate patterns change in various areas.[9] They speculate that local animal, plant, and insect populations could be affected by weather changes as well. That could make it hard (or impossible) for some kinds of those animals, plants, or insects to survive in their normal habitat. Some species might die off, while other species might migrate into areas where the weather is more to their liking. But this change in what investigators call the "home range" of various animal and insect populations has a dark side. Such movements might lead to people being exposed to diseases carried by insect pests that were previously uncommon to their area.[10]

But understanding why the earth's temperature changes is difficult, because unlike an oven or a room, the earth's average temperature is not controlled by a simple thermostat. Instead, a web of heating and cooling forces interact in a complex way to set the average temperature at the surface of the earth, and local weather patterns lead to local temperature patterns that shift back and forth around that average.

While investigators understand how some of these forces work, many remain a mystery. But overall, the interaction of those many climate forces leads sometimes to periods of warmth and other times to periods of coolness.

Some of those heating and cooling forces include:

- sunlight that reaches the earth from the sun

- heat reflected back into space from the surface of the earth

- heat trapped by gases in the atmosphere

- heat trapped by water vapor in the atmosphere

- heat reflected upward or downward by clouds

- heat absorbed and re-emitted by oceans; and more.

To make a complicated issue even more complicated, many of these climate forces change over time, and some of them can influence one another, sometimes positively, sometimes negatively. For example, some heat patterns change due to the irregular nature of the earth's orbit. Rather than orbiting around the sun in a perfect circle year after year, the earth's orbit is somewhat irregular, which means that for some spans of time, the earth averages a little closer into the sun, and at other times, it is a little bit farther away. The amount of sunlight the earth receives changes accordingly. The earth also wobbles in its orbit around the sun, changing which part of the earth faces in toward the sun most directly. Other forces vary simply because the sun does not burn at the same level all the time—when it burns hotter or cooler, the earth has more or less energy pumped into the climate.

While a great deal is known about how the earth's temperature is regulated, there is a lot more to learn. While some climate investigators think enough is known about how the climate works to start making changes in the way humans affect it, others disagree. Some investigators think it will be another fifty years before human understanding of the climate will be highly accurate and can allow us to make reliable predictions about how the future climate may change.

3

Hard Evidence of Global Warming

After the wacky hot weather of 1988, investigators quickly found a "suspect" in the case of the warming planet. James Hansen and others quickly pointed the finger of suspicion at the greenhouse gases humanity has added to the atmosphere. But having a suspect and being sure that it is the right suspect are two different things. It took several hundred years to formulate the theory of global warming, but now investigators faced a more difficult challenge: gathering evidence and trying to figure out what it all meant. And while it is easy to ask

38

whether human action is causing the climate to change, the question is much easier to ask than it is to answer.

Climate investigators quickly found out how complicated the job would be when they looked for the answer to the first major question of global warming: Has the temperature at the earth's surface warmed up in an unnatural way in recent years? Actually, investigators had to answer a difficult question even before that. How do you take the temperature of an entire planet?

Researchers quickly realized that measuring the temperature of the earth was more than just taking a few temperature readings. In fact, figuring out the average temperature of the earth's atmosphere is incredibly complicated. Calculating the temperature of a large space (such as the oceans, the earth's surface layers, and the earth's atmosphere) is much harder than taking the temperature of a smaller object, or a person, or measuring the temperature of a pot of water.

Taking a Room's Temperature

Consider a familiar example. How would you take the "average" temperature of the air in a classroom? You could start by simply putting a thermometer in the middle of the room and seeing what it says. But do we know if the temperature there is the same as near the wall? But if you want to measure against a wall, which wall would be best? And what height on the wall do you hold it against? Do you put it near

Changes in the temperature of the ocean could adversely affect fish and animals such as this pilot whale (top) and bottlenose dolphin.

the ceiling, near the floor, or at the exact middle of the wall? Even small rooms can have major differences in temperature for a variety of reasons. Because hot air rises, for example, a temperature reading taken up by the ceiling would probably be higher than a reading taken down near the floor. You would probably expect a higher temperature reading near the window on a hot summer day than you would against the opposite wall. You would certainly expect a higher temperature reading with the thermometer in direct sunlight than you would if it were in the shade. If there are air conditioners or heaters running, the blowing air will create different temperature zones closer to, and farther from the vents. If you were holding the thermometer near a dark-painted wall, rather than a light-painted wall, the temperature reading would be higher since dark surfaces absorb more heat than light ones. And if you took a single reading, how much of the room would that reading really represent? Is all the air within a foot of the floor the same temperature? What about the air within two feet of the floor, or up near the ceiling?

It is pretty clear that to really calculate the temperature of a whole room, you would have to take many temperature readings, figure out how much of the room each of those readings represented, and then use a lot of math to average the many readings of the many different temperature zones throughout the room. As you can see, calculating the average temperature of even such a small space as a classroom is not as simple as it might seem upon first inspection.

But temperature differences based on the location of the thermometer are only one factor. To tell whether the temperature is changing over time, as investigators need to know for climate studies, one would have to take repeated measurements throughout the room and do those averaging calculations time after time. So to see whether that classroom was showing warmer temperatures over time, you would have to take many repeated measurements. And it is still more complicated if you want to know whether the temperature readings you are taking are abnormal for that particular time of year. In measuring that classroom, you would also have to pick times that reflect the overall pattern of temperature change, and not pick times that only show extremes like the hottest minute or the coldest one.

Trying to calculate an average temperature and track how it changes over time would pose a serious challenge even for a single room. And such a measurement would still only tell you part of the story; it would not reflect the way the heat of objects within the room might change, such as the walls, the floor, the ceiling, or the desks. It would not tell you how the plants, animals, or people in the room would react to the changing temperatures either. And even knowing the temperature, its trend, and its "normality" would not necessarily tell you the best way to change things more to your liking.

When you consider the complications in figuring all this out for just one classroom, it becomes obvious that answering the question "Is the earth warming?" is far harder than asking it. But when the unusually hot summer of 1988 rekindled interest in the theory of global warming, that was the question climate investigators knew was first on the list. Was the warming that was being observed due to human action, or was it just a natural variation of the sort that the earth experiences all the time?

Well aware of the difficulties involved, climate investigators started their search for an answer by digging into the evidence most readily at hand, the records of temperature and weather kept over the years at weather stations from all over the earth. For over 150 years, people have taken temperature readings at these weather stations, giving climate investigators four main sets of temperature readings to work with in looking at the trends in the atmosphere's average temperature. The four sets consist of temperature readings taken at weather stations on the ground, temperature readings taken on ships at sea, temperature readings taken from floating weather balloons, and temperature readings taken by satellites orbiting the earth.

Ground-based Temperature Measurements

The biggest set of temperature readings investigators use to study whether the atmosphere is warming are taken using regular glass thermometers at land-based weather stations. Until the recent development of electronic thermometers, these readings were taken with the same kind of glass thermometers people use to measure the temperature of the air in their living room or the water in a pool. Currently, there are millions of individual temperature measurements being taken every year using regular glass thermometers at over eight thousand weather stations all around the world.[1]

The process of joining all those temperature readings together and calculating an average global temperature is a huge challenge. As discussed earlier, for even a single room, you would have to make assumptions about how much of the room a given thermometer reading really represents. With its widely varied temperature zones and patterns, the earth's surface is many times more complicated than a single room.

Figure 2 shows how the earth's average temperature has changed over the last 150 years. Since the temperature of the atmosphere can fluctuate by more than 50 degrees in a single day at some spots on the earth, climate investigators perform a calculation that lets them express an area's temperature by the way it differs from the average temperature for that time and place observed over a long span of time, such as thirty years. These values are called "temperature anomalies." Temperature anomalies do not represent the actual temperature; they just say whether the temperature was warmer than average or colder than average for the time the measurement was taken.

Some climate investigators argue that the trend shown in this graph indicates that the earth's atmosphere is warming up over time. In their last published report, IPCC investigators said their research indicates that temperatures recorded at measuring stations on the ground reveal an average warming ranging from 0.4°C to 0.8°C since the year 1850. That is, the average temperature of the atmosphere near the earth's surface in the year 2000 was between 0.4° and 0.8° warmer than it was during the year 1850.

One half to one third of this warming, according to the investigators, has happened since the mid-1970s. But the IPCC investigators point out that

FIGURE 2: Global Annual Temperature Anomalies, 1850–2010[2]

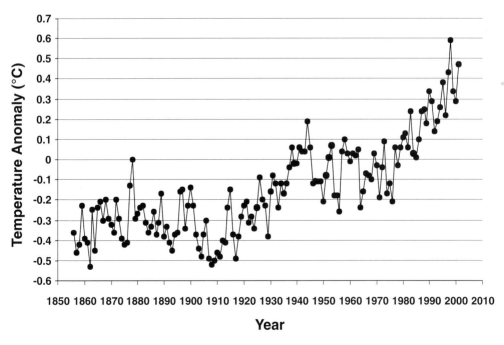

the warming of the earth's average temperature has not caused a uniform amount of warming to happen everywhere around the earth. Some parts of the earth have warmed up more than others. For example, more of the warming seen since 1850 has happened over land rather than over water. And the warming is not spread out evenly over the course of the day or night. In fact, more of the warming seen since 1850 has happened at night. The warming also shows up mostly during an area's winter. So, instead of making for warmer summertime days, the warming since 1850 has made mostly for slightly warmer wintertime nights. Finally, more of the warming since 1850 has happened over the high-latitude parts of the earth, particularly in the north, rather than over areas closer to the equator.

But some climate investigators inside and outside the IPCC have conflicting ideas about the meaning of all these changes. For example, some scientists have pointed out that 150 years worth of temperature records are not that useful when the earth's climate has been evolving and changing for 4 billion years.[3] To understand how short a stretch of history 150 years is, consider this thought experiment. If you squeezed all of the earth's history into a single twenty-four-hour period, humanity's direct measurement of the temperature would only cover the last three one thousandths of a second. That is far less time than it takes for the blink of a human eye. Even one thousand years of temperature readings would equate to only two hundredths of the last second.[4]

With a short set of temperature readings, and a

very long pattern of temperature change, it is hard to know whether the increase of the last one hundred years or so is part of a long-term trend or is just a short-term rise in temperatures. Such short-term warm-ups have happened before as a natural part of the earth's temperature cycle from ice ages to warm periods.

And then, as some climate investigators have observed, many of the temperature records suffer from accuracy problems. Thermometers used in taking older recordings were primitive by modern standards, some even having hand-painted number scales. And since the people taking the temperature readings were not all working together, they did not collect temperatures in a way that would shed the most light on the temperature of the entire earth. For one thing, not all the temperature readings were taken in the same way. Some readings were taken in the sun, while some were taken in the shade. In some cases, the thermometer was moved around, in others, it was always in the same position. Some weather stations only recorded the temperature for a short period of time, while others recorded for longer.

But the biggest problem with the record of temperatures taken on land is that most of the readings were taken near cities, and cities, as Hume pointed out, can change the local temperature all by themselves.[5] Hume had not identified the different factors that cause a city to be warmer than the surrounding countryside, but modern scientists have. Because they have fewer trees to shade them and more dark-colored paved surfaces, cities tend to absorb heat during the daytime more than surrounding, less developed areas do. This effect, called the "urban heat island" effect, is what keeps a city warmer than the countryside around it.[6]

Some climate investigators argue that the mathematical process used to average all the individual surface temperature readings exaggerates the warming because most of the readings were taken in cities, which tend to be hotter than surrounding areas.[7] IPCC investigators, on the other hand, claim to have accounted for the urban heat island effect and argue that the surface temperature record is an accurate reflection of temperature changes that have occurred over the last 150 years. But the research continues, even on this basic question about the meaning of thermometer readings.

Temperature Measurements from Weather Balloons, Ships, and Satellites

Temperature readings of both the water and the air were also taken on ships traveling the oceans, for a variety of uses. These temperature records span nearly the same time as the land-based readings, but they are not as useful for charting the earth's temperature as the land-based reading for many reasons.

Recording Temperatures at Sea. It is even more complicated to take the temperature of the air when you are on a ship at sea than it is when you are on the ground in a city. For one thing, until very recently, ships did not know their exact locations on the surface of the earth, unless they were in a port.

URBAN HEAT ISLANDS

What is an urban heat island? Climate investigators studying temperature records noticed an interesting thing: Temperatures taken in cities tend to be higher than temperatures taken in rural settings, even when the thermometers are located only a few miles apart. This effect is illustrated graphically in the picture below.

In fact, cities may be as much as 6° C to 8° C hotter than the surrounding countryside. Cities are so hot because of all the dark-colored surfacing materials used in roads and buildings and the reduction in tree cover that often goes along with building houses, roads, office buildings, and so on.

Urban Heat Island Profile[8]

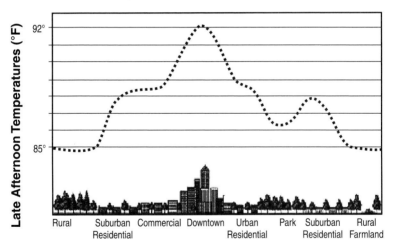

When climate investigators first started studying temperature recordings to see if the earth was warming, they were unaware of this effect, and, since most temperature records had been taken in the middle of urban heat islands, early estimates were biased, showing greater warming than was actually the case.

Once a ship took to sea and went beyond the sight of land, ship captains could record their position on the globe only roughly, by calculating their latitude and longitude. That inability to know exactly where they were is important because the temperature of the earth changes from place to place, even over the ocean and even over only a few dozen miles. And there were other complicating factors as well. As climate researchers found when they started looking into the accuracy of ocean-based temperature readings, the changes in technology were even more dramatic at sea than they were on land. Before 1940, for example, ocean water temperatures were taken by having sailors pull buckets of water out of the ocean. Sailors would then stick a thermometer in the bucket and take the temperature of the water while the bucket was sitting on the deck of the ship. Investigators looked at these recordings partly to learn about the temperature of the water itself but also to learn about the temperature of the air above the water.

But one complication arose right away. As sailors pulled the water bucket up and left it sitting on the deck of the ship, the temperature of the water could change depending on whether it was cloudy or bright, windy or still. And if the bucket was put in a shaded place, it would cool faster than in a sunny place on deck. Even the direction the ship was traveling in could change the temperature readings, because the wind might blow differently depending on which way the ship was pointed with respect to the wind. But those were only the obvious problems investigators found with the temperature readings. When looking still further, scientists found that the temperature reading of the water also changed depending on what kind of bucket was used. When pulling the bucket of water up out of the ocean, air flowing by the bucket would chill the water inside. This evaporative cooling is how some types of home air conditioners work, and it is also how your body cools down when you sweat and stand in the breeze. Climate investigators found that if the bucket the sailors used was made with canvas, this evaporative cooling effect would be greater than the cooling that would happen if they had used a metal, wood, or plastic bucket.

Similar problems affected the normal air-based temperature readings taken on ships. As with water temperature readings, air readings were not always taken at the same places on the earth. But even where they were, there was a problem. Because the ships themselves got bigger over time, the sailors standing on the deck recording the air temperature were actually taking temperatures farther above the surface of the ocean than previous sailors had, even if they were in the very same place.

Weather Balloons. Climate researchers have some more modern sets of temperature recordings taken since the 1960s, when some high-technology approaches to tracking the weather became more commonplace. Since the 1960s, for example, temperatures of the air have not only been taken at ground level, but they have also been taken with thermometers and other temperature-measuring devices mounted on weather balloons.

But even these modern records are limited in the information they tell climate researchers about the global temperature. The biggest limitation of weather balloons, like that of surface temperature readings, is that they only measure the temperature over certain parts of the world, namely, where weather stations sent them up. Though they do drift away from where they are launched, balloons have not been sent up to all parts of the atmosphere evenly, nor over extended periods of time. Balloons were used, originally, to detect local temperatures in order to predict short-term weather, not long-term trends in the climate. Thus, depending on what kind of information was most desired, balloons were sent up to different heights, were kept up for different periods of time, were flown at different times of the day or night, and were flown over only a tiny fraction of the earth's surface, namely, where people lived and had weather research stations. Further complicating things, balloons also had different kinds of thermometers and radio equipment used at different times and places, making temperature readings hard to compare with each other. And of course, the balloon readings can record the temperature at certain heights, but figuring out how the temperature varies between that measurement point and the ground poses still another challenge.

Satellites. The most recently assembled, and most high-tech, set of direct temperature readings comes from satellites that orbit the earth. These satellites record the temperature of the atmosphere using special cameras that measure the heat given off by the upper layers of the earth's atmosphere. Satellite temperature readings are the first ones that can actually measure the temperature of the entire atmosphere at different heights. Such global satellite temperature readings have been taken nearly continuously since 1979. Still, as some climate investigators point out, the satellite temperature readings have their shortcomings. Just like land-based and ocean-based temperature recordings, satellite recording devices have changed over time. Newer devices do not measure the temperature in exactly the same way as previous devices did. Furthermore, satellites do not stay in orbit forever. Eventually, the satellites spiral down toward the earth and burn up in the atmosphere. Indeed, when they looked more closely, climate investigators found that the temperature readings taken by satellites change as they slowly spiral in toward the earth. Because of the way the satellites take the temperature of the atmosphere, the readings depend on how far away the satellite is from the earth. Temperature readings taken from closer into the earth are lower than readings of the same place on the earth's surface when taken from a higher orbit.

And aside from technology changes, climate investigators differ over the real meaning of land-based, water-based, satellite, and balloon temperature recordings. As discussed above, it is hard to know what the slight warming seen in the temperature records taken on the land really means, because the land-based temperature record is so short compared to the long history of earth's climate. Temperatures taken from weather balloons and satellites span an even shorter period than the surface temperature readings or ocean temperature readings do. Further complicating the picture is the fact that the newest temperature readings from satellites and balloons do not tend to match up well with the readings taken on the land or at sea. While the surface and ocean temperature records tend to match up pretty well with each other, and the satellite and balloon temperature readings match up with each other, the readings taken from higher up disagree with the readings taken near the earth's surface. Figure 3 shows how the three main sets of temperature recordings match up over time.

As you can see, though the surface temperature readings suggest that the earth is warming near the ground, the satellite and balloon evidence suggests that little or no warming has happened higher up in the atmosphere. Some investigators feel that this difference in recorded temperature trends is meaningful, while others disagree.

John Christy, a climate investigator who takes such satellite readings, is one of those investigators arguing that the satellite temperature record shows that something is wrong with the current scientific understanding of global warming. Christy claims that if the scientific theories used to understand all of the complicated climate processes on earth are correct, then the satellite readings should not show a cooling trend. Christy and others argue that the disagreement between the different temperature records means there is something missing in the basic theory of global warming.[9]

But in a report by the United States National Academy of Sciences (NAS), a highly respected panel of investigators argued that the difference between ground, balloon, and satellite measurements does not indicate a real problem with global warming theory. The NAS argues that while the surface and satellite

FIGURE 3: Temperature Anomalies from Surface,[10] Satellite,[11] and Weather Balloon[12] Measurements, 1978–2002

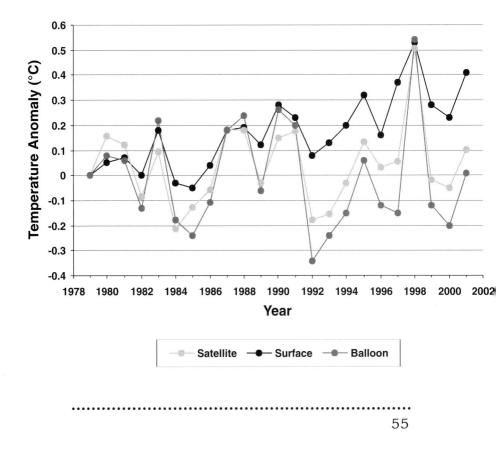

temperatures disagree with each other and with some of the theories of how earth's climate really works, the differences in the two temperature records do not mean that either of them are wrong, only that science has not yet explained why they could differ.[13]

Other Sources of Temperature Estimates

Climate investigators studying global temperatures would be in trouble if the only evidence they had was the direct temperature readings discussed in the previous section. For one thing, they would be stuck with only 150 years of data, from which they would be trying to understand trends lasting hundreds or thousands of years. Fortunately, there are ways to estimate past temperatures, even though nobody was around to take measurements at the time.

Boreholes and Ice Cores. One way that climate investigators can estimate the temperature from the past, before there were temperature readings to rely on, is through the examination of something called a borehole. A borehole is made when scientists bore a deep cylinder-shaped hole in ice, soil, or mud. Scientists can use such holes to estimate what the temperature must have been long ago. And by studying the long cylinders of ice that can be pulled out of glaciers (called ice cores), scientists can learn even more about the climate of the past.

Climate investigators have found that boreholes can be used to estimate temperatures from long ago, because heating and cooling of things follow predictable trends over time. If you think about it, things do not heat up or cool down all at once; it takes time. Even things like soil, rock, and ice heat up and cool down over time in a predictable way. So how do scientists tell the temperature of the past by looking at the inside of a hole? They do it by understanding that glaciers, and the other solid surfaces on the earth, were made more recently than the parts deeper down. Just as you dig down in the earth to find fossils and things that lived long ago, so scientists can dig down into the earth and find out what the temperature was at times in the distant past.

After drilling a borehole into a glacier, a lake

Ice cores provide information on the climate of the past. Shown are researchers in Antarctica with ice-coring equipment.

bottom, or regular soil, scientists lower sensitive thermometers into the hole and measure the temperature at different depths. For ice, for the muck at the bottom of a river, and even for regular soil, deeper layers are a reflection of the past, and they can be used to estimate the temperature of the surface at that time. By examining the fossils found at those different depths, climate investigators can estimate which depth matches up with a certain time in the past and can estimate what the temperature was thousands and even hundreds of thousands of years ago.

Over six hundred such boreholes have been drilled around the world in efforts to chart what the local temperatures were before humans started taking measurements with thermometers.

Besides simply boring holes into ice, climate investigators can learn a lot about the past climate by drilling out long, thin cylinders of ice called ice cores. By pulling tiny bubbles of air out of the ice cores from depths matching up with times in the past, climate investigators can measure the types of gas found in the atmosphere at the time, including the greenhouse gas, carbon dioxide. With such information, climate investigators can not only study the temperature but can also track how past temperatures match up with historical levels of carbon dioxide and use that information to test the theory of global warming. Most such studies of ice cores suggest that higher levels of carbon dioxide happen nearly at the same time as increases in temperature, but some studies suggest that it is not always so.[14]

Climate researchers studying temperature measurements taken from boreholes suggest their findings agree with the thermometer readings of the last 150 years and show the warming goes a bit further back as well. Their findings indicate that the earth's atmosphere is growing a bit warmer and has increased in average temperature by about 1° C over the last 150 years.[15]

But when scientists estimate ancient temperatures from boreholes, they have to be very careful that the holes were not contaminated during the drilling process, and they have to make many assumptions. They make assumptions about how fast heat travels through ice and about whether gas bubbles retain the same concentrations of gases that they had so many thousands of years ago.[16] As the IPCC's newest report points out, many things can interfere with the relationship between ice core readings and the actual surface temperature. For example, when humans change the environment, replacing natural land cover of shrubs or trees with planted crops, for example, they can cause changes in the winter snow cover and soil moisture of areas nearby. The same is true when people build cities where there once were prairies, forests, or swamps. And over time, as human societies moved around, the changes they made in the environment could make the borehole temperature readings less accurate. And other investigators have pointed to deeper problems with information gathered from ice cores and boreholes. The biggest riddle is that sometimes the temperature seems to match up with carbon dioxide levels, and sometimes it does not.

If carbon dioxide was causing global warming, we would expect the carbon dioxide level to rise first and then the temperature to rise second. But studies of ice cores show that sometimes, the temperature and carbon dioxide go up in tandem, yet other times, carbon dioxide goes up first, and the temperature increase lags, by up to one thousand years. Sometimes, the temperature goes up first, and the carbon dioxide follows.[17]

The relationship between changes in the level of greenhouse gases and changes in the temperature is an important issue in understanding global warming. If the theory of global warming is correct, and changing levels of gases like carbon dioxide cause the earth's temperature to warm or cool, records should show that carbon dioxide levels rise before the earth starts to warm, and not vice versa. And if historical temperature readings from ice cores and boreholes show that the earth's temperature changed more in the past than people assume today, then current temperature patterns might not be abnormal, and the search for a human cause for global warming might be a search in the wrong direction.

Tree Rings. The way trees grow depends on many different things, but one important factor is the temperature. Trees grow faster when it is warm than they do when it is cold, and as they grow, trees produce "rings" that preserve information about how warm or how cold it was during a given growing season. Because trees grow differently based on local climate conditions, tree ring records say more about local changes in climate than they do about the earth as a whole.

Climate investigators looking at tree rings have estimated what the temperature was as far back as the oldest living trees, all the way back to 1000 A.D. for some tree species. Figure 4 shows an estimated temperature record in the Gulf of Alaska for the period from 1732 through 1980, based on tree-ring growth patterns.

Investigators studying tree-ring growth patterns in the Northern Hemisphere have shown that the twentieth century was somewhat warmer than average. Studies of tree rings in the Southern Hemisphere offer a more confusing picture: In some places, tree rings reflect warmer-than-average temperatures for the twentieth century, while in other places, tree rings indicate that temperatures were no warmer than average.

FIGURE 4: Temperature Estimates Based on Tree Rings, 1732–1980[18]

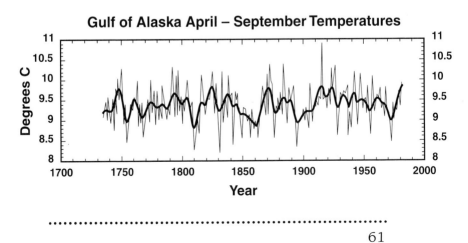

Gulf of Alaska April – September Temperatures

Tree rings can indicate weather conditions back hundreds of years.

Of course, as with the other evidence discussed above, tree-ring records are of limited use to climate investigators. For one thing, trees grow only on land, and they have to be quite old to tell investigators about the temperature of the more distant past. As climate investigators have found, trees that big and old are not very plentiful. And even when the right tree is found, tree-ring patterns can sometimes lead to false conclusions about the local weather. Out by the coast, for example, ocean currents and other climate factors can produce local temperatures that are not always reflective of the region as a whole, so figuring out whether the tree rings really represent the temperature of a significant area is tricky. And then, tree-ring evidence poses many other problems for climate investigators, since the rings represent not only temperature, but also rainfall and other factors.[19]

Corals. Still another place that climate investigators look for information about past climate conditions is out in the oceans—or areas that used to be oceans. Climate investigators found that when shell-bearing ocean animals (such as coral) make their shells, the minerals they use vary with the temperature of the water. The temperature of the water, in turn, is related to the temperature of the air. Corals are tiny invertebrates that build their shells on top of the shells left behind by earlier shell-makers. Because the minerals used in making those older coral shells reflected ocean conditions at the time, they are like little recordings of what ocean conditions and temperature were at the time they were made. Since

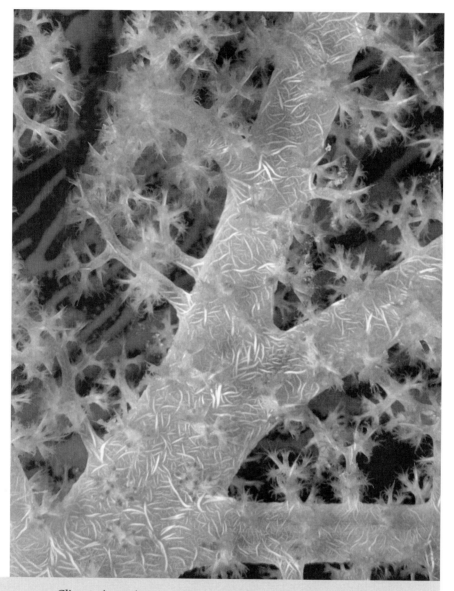

Climate investigators examine coral, such as this lavender soft coral tree, for information about past climate conditions in the ocean.

corals grow upward, toward the light, older layers are farther down in the ocean. By looking at the different elements incorporated into ocean coral (and the bands of color that match up with past periods of warmth), climate investigators can estimate the temperature of the water from thousands of years in the past.

In general, evidence about past temperatures from the study of corals matches up well with tree rings in estimating past temperatures, and both temperature histories suggest a recent global warming. But as with tree rings, there are limits to the usefulness of coral-based temperature estimates. While temperature is one factor involved in the way that corals build their shells, other factors are also involved, such as the saltiness of the water, the presence of nutrients that corals need to build their shells, and the presence of other minerals dissolved in the water. Diseases and long-term ocean current patterns like El Niño and La Niña can strongly affect coral growth patterns as well. And, like tree rings, corals are not distributed evenly around the world, and those useful for taking temperature readings are from selected places and may not reflect the temperature of the rest of the earth very well.

4

Circumstantial Evidence of Global Warming

Aside from temperature readings and fossil evidence, global warming theory suggests that changes in the earth's average temperature should cause other weather changes to occur as well. And because such changes would include big weather systems and easily measured phenomenon like rainfall, snowfall, and so on, they might be more easily measured than the underlying temperature change by itself.

Changes in rainfall levels, snowfall levels, iceberg numbers and locations, polar ice caps, and the strength or frequency of storms have all been proposed as circumstantial evidence of global warming. Climate investigators trying to determine whether the earth's average temperature is changing also monitor these climate trends and ask whether they show evidence of changes in average temperature and whether those changes match up with the changes suggested by direct temperature readings discussed above.

Rainfall Evidence

According to global warming theory, increased temperatures should speed up the cycle of evaporation and rainfall that scientists call the "hydrologic cycle." That increased speed, climate investigators suspect, should lead to increased rainfall. Of course, not all areas would experience the same thing, because many different forces control rainfall, including wind patterns, humidity levels, and the shape of the land.

Clear changes in rainfall trends could provide additional evidence that could help climate investigators decide whether the earth is currently experiencing a warming trend. But according to the IPCC investigators, the trends in rainfall have been mixed. Though more than twenty thousand weather stations have recorded rainfall levels, trends in rainfall are hard to spot. Over land, IPCC investigators think that rainfall has increased by about 2 percent since the beginning of the twentieth century, but the distribution of the change has varied around the earth.

During the twentieth century, for example, rainfall increased between 9 percent and 16 percent over the parts of the earth above the equator, from 35° N to 85° N latitude. During that same time, rainfall levels increased between 2 percent and 5 percent in the band below the equator, from 0° S to 55° S latitude.

Regionally, though, patterns are harder to see. Rainfall over the United States, for example, has increased between 5 percent and 10 percent since 1900, but there have been long periods of drought as well, such as those during the 1930s and 1950s. Over Canada, rainfall has increased over 10 percent during the twentieth century, while over China, the last 50 years have seen a decrease in annual rainfall. Over the area that used to be called the Soviet Union, rainfall has increased over the twentieth century.

Like the temperature trends discussed above, changes in rainfall are happening unevenly both geographically and over time. Complicating the situation, the places receiving more or less rainfall do not necessarily match up with the places experiencing temperatures that are warmer or cooler than average, so it is hard to tell if changes in temperature are causing the changes in rainfall.

Besides serving as indirect evidence of global warming, tracking rainfall patterns is important for another reason: If the earth is warming up, harmful consequences will be tied, in large part, to changes in rainfall. Floods, droughts, and even very heavy rains can significantly interfere with activities such as farming, construction, and transportation. Heavy rains can also cause massive property damage when cities and towns are flooded, and in extreme cases, such flooding can even kill people.

Investigators believe that global warming should cause more rainfall; however, a clear increase has not been found.

But IPCC investigators note that records of rainfall have as many problems as temperature records do, if not more. They point out that records of rainfall cover only certain areas for certain periods of time, are not all taken with the same accuracy or equipment, are subject to changes because of the wind, and do not always have information about the extent of rainfall in the area around the rain gauge.[1]

It is hard to tell from looking at records of precipitation whether or not the climate has changed to reflect global warming. Investigators will need to gather more evidence before they can use rainfall records to help them decide whether the temperature record they have is correct or not.

Sea-Level Evidence

Besides looking to the skies, climate investigators can also look to the sea for supporting evidence of global warming. Global warming theory suggests that rising global temperatures would cause sea levels to rise because water expands more when it is hot than when it is cold. On top of that thermal expansion, melting glaciers, snow packs, and parts of the polar ice caps now on the land would add water to the oceans and raise the level as well.

As glaciers have melted since the last ice age, the seas have risen dramatically. Since the last glacial maximum (18,000 to 22,000 years ago, when glaciers covered much of the earth), sea level has risen by over 120 meters at locations near and far from the now-melted glaciers. Investigators have also shown that the sea level rose sharply between fifteen thousand and six thousand years ago, when sea levels rose at an average rate of 10 millimeters (mm) (a little over 4 inches) per year. Sea level rise slowed down somewhat from six thousand to three thousand years ago, only rising at about 0.4 to 0.6 mm (less than $^1/_{16}$ of an inch) each year, and from about three thousand years ago until recently, sea level rise was slower still, at only about 0.1 to 0.2 mm per year.[2]

Recent amounts of sea level rise might not seem like a lot, but small changes in sea level can mean big changes for people and animals living in and near the ocean. Not only can rising sea levels flood coastal properties, they can also force salty ocean water underground, contaminating local fresh water supplies and changing the saltiness of freshwater estuaries, affecting local fish and bird populations.

Some recent studies of sea levels indicate an increase in the rate of sea level rise, estimated to be between 100 and 200 millimeters (between 4 and 8 inches) over the last hundred years. However, there is a lot of doubt attached to that figure, because the land also rises and falls due to underground activity, and ocean currents change as well. Adding to the confusion is the fact that because sea level changes so slowly, short-term records are not as accurate as long-term records. And different parts of the earth's oceans rise at different rates because of their underwater landscape, further complicating the picture. Finally, several trends have climate investigators scratching their heads. For some parts of the world, such as Antarctica and Greenland, evidence suggests that the level of the ocean has actually dropped.[3] And though the rate of global warming has theoretically been speeding up, there is little evidence that the rate of sea-level rise has sped up to match, as theory would suggest. Though warming and glacial melting have both supposedly sped up in the twentieth century, the sea level did not rise at a faster rate in the twentieth century than in the nineteenth century.[4]

As with rainfall records, evidence about changes in sea level are not really strong enough to tell climate investigators whether the earth's surface is really warming as the various temperature readings discussed earlier suggest. More evidence, gathered over a longer period of time, will be needed before sea-level change will be useful in validating the evidence gathered by thermometers, weather balloons, and satellites.

Surface-Water Evidence

Global warming would also be expected to influence bodies of "surface water" such as lakes and streams, in a similar way to the oceans. Not only would the water in the streams and rivers expand, but changing rainfall and snow patterns would also affect the water level. More or less rain would raise or lower the levels of streams and lakes, as well as increasing or decreasing the usefulness of underground bodies of water called aquifers. Many people get their drinking water from such surface and subsurface water supplies, and if too little rain falls, those aquifers and rivers can run out of usable water, forcing people to have water imported from other places, often a very expensive proposition.

But IPCC investigators report no clear evidence that stream flows are changing, either over the course of the year or during peak periods of stream flow after major storms.[5] While the levels of lakes and inland seas (such as the Caspian Sea) have varied over time, IPCC researchers point out that local weather effects can change the level of lakes and inland seas, making them unreliable as indicators of global changes.

Snow Evidence

Global warming affects more than just the temperature. Because of its effects on things like cloudiness, humidity, and weather circulation patterns, global warming would also be expected to influence things like the rate of snowfall, the total snow depth that falls in a year, and the amount of the world covered by snow in any given year.

As with so many other elements of global warming, however, studies examining changes in these snow characteristics show mixed evidence. Snow cover (the total area covered by snow) has declined in recent years, with a higher percentage of moisture in cold areas coming down as rain, rather than snow. That is what one would expect if it really is warming up, as the temperature records discussed above suggest.

But while the area covered by snow in the Northern Hemisphere has declined by about 10 percent over the past thirty-six years, some areas have actually gotten more snowfall than usual. And while the extent of snow cover has fallen in the spring, it has actually increased during winter, which is when the largest share of global warming is apparent.[6]

Like the other climate trends discussed above, changes in snowfall are not spread evenly around the earth. Rather than decreasing, snow extent has increased in some parts of the world, even as the earth warms.[7] Observed changes in snowfall are not consistent in time, either. Snowfall over China decreased during the 1950s but increased during the 1960s and 1970s.

Besides the area of the earth covered by snow in a given year, global warming would be expected to change the average depth of snow as well. Some parts of the world have experienced deeper-than-average snowfall in recent years, while other parts have not. For example, snow-depth measurements in the former Soviet Union over the twentieth century show decreased snow depth of about 14 percent during the winter, mostly in the Western portion of the ex-Union. But for nearly half of that time, from the 1960s on, the Eastern parts of the ex-Union were having decreasing snow depths.

Ice-Mass Evidence

The earth has many masses of ice in cold areas, including glaciers, ice caps, ice sheets, and sea ice (such as icebergs). The evidence available to climate investigators regarding changes in glaciers and ice caps is very limited. From the records of explorers, climate investigators know that many of the world's glaciers have clearly shrunk over the last hundred years. But scientists differ over when that shrinkage started, and, therefore, its relationship to global warming.[8]

In fact, as the IPCC investigators point out, evidence of ice-sheet change is actually contradictory: Some evidence suggests that the Greenland and Antarctic ice sheets are shrinking. Other evidence suggests they are growing. Still other evidence suggests that some ice sheets, such as the Greenland ice sheet, may be doing both, growing on top and shrinking at the edges.[9]

Finally, regarding floating sea-ice masses such as icebergs, the evidence collected by climate

Scientists have found contradictory evidence about changes in ice mass; some appears to be increasing, while some appears to be shrinking. Shown is an iceberg off Baffin Island in the Northwest Territories, Canada.

investigators suggests that sea ice is covering a smaller part of the Arctic oceans than during spring and summer months, compared to the historical average. During the arctic summer, sea-ice levels do not seem to have changed from their historical patterns. In Antarctica, by contrast, there is no clear trend in the coverage of the ocean by sea ice since 1973, when satellite measurements first began.[10]

It is clear that more evidence will have to be gathered before changes in glaciers and ice sheets can be used to determine if the earth is actually warming, as temperature records suggest.

Evidence of Changes in Severe Weather

Finally, as with a pot of water on the stove, heating up the atmosphere would be expected to cause an increase in the severity or changeability of weather. Finding such changes would give researchers still another form of indirect evidence reflecting whether the earth is currently undergoing climate change.

And some researchers have looked for such evidence, after predicting that a warmer world would also have more frequent bouts of extreme weather, including heat waves, cold snaps, tornadoes, thunderstorms, dust storms and so on. But so far, there is not much evidence supporting these predictions on a global scale.

IPCC climate investigators conclude in their most recent report: "No systematic changes in the frequency of tornadoes, thunder days, or hail events are evident in the limited areas analysed."[11] They observe that at local levels, some areas have experienced more extreme or more rapidly changing weather, but the evidence is mixed: Some of the changes have been toward more rapid changeability than usual, and some have been toward less rapid changeability.[12] Because of limited information, it is unclear whether tropical storms or other kinds of dangerous weather phenomena are increasing, as they would be expected to do in a warmer world.

Sifting a Mountain of Evidence

Since the unusually hot summer of 1988, climate investigators have been on a quest to determine

Researchers say that a rise in atmospheric temperature should result in an increase in severe weather events. Shown is a photo of a hurricane taken from space.

whether the earth is heating up in an ongoing way because of human action. To answer that question, researchers have gathered a massive amount of direct and circumstantial evidence, from thermometers, weather balloons, satellites, boreholes, ice cores, tree rings, rainfall readings, snowfall readings, icebergs, glaciers, and more.

Though the majority of climate investigators are agreed that the earth has warmed a bit at the surface in recent years, the cause of that warming and its impacts on other types of climate phenomena are less clear. Trends in rainfall are mixed, as are trends in snowfall. Trends in sea-level rise are not conclusive, nor are trends in extreme weather events. Trends in the melting of glacial ice are in line with a continued warming of the earth since the last ice age, but even this trend is confusing, with some areas of the earth experiencing the growth of glaciers, even while the temperature is going up.

Still, most climate investigators interpret the observed changes in these climate measurements as suggesting that the earth is warming up in an unusual way, and they suspect the influence of humanity. Others find the evidence unconvincing, and note alternative explanations for the recent changes that have been observed. Some say that we may only be suffering from an overly short-term point of view, pointing to earlier fluctuations in earth's temperature that make the recent changes seem minor by comparison.[13]

5

The Primary Suspects— Greenhouse Gases

Among those who feel that the globe is warming, different climate investigators propose different suspects. Some investigators say human action is responsible, some say that other causes lie behind the warming. Some investigators think that only one human activity is responsible, while other investigators point to a different, mutually exclusive activity. Everywhere one turns, the evidence is mixed.

Assigning responsibility for global warming is tricky and is based more on circumstantial evidence drawn from scientific theories and computer models than on hard evidence. Why do some people think humans are warming the globe? Why do others think humans are not to blame? What do investigators think is the cause of recent changes in climate?

To understand the answers to such questions, one has to understand the nature of earth's atmosphere and the gases that make it up. The atmosphere is the layer of gases that surrounds the earth. The atmosphere is composed mostly of nitrogen and oxygen, but there are smaller quantities of other gases mixed in. Because most of these gases are transparent, we do not think about them very much, certainly not as something that affects the average temperature of the earth's surface. However, as we discussed earlier, several of the gases in the earth's atmosphere—the greenhouse gases—play a key role in setting the thermostat of the earth's surface. The different gases found in the atmosphere, as Fourier showed, trap heat in different ways.

Scientists talk about the gases in the atmosphere using terms like "parts per million" and "parts per billion." Sometimes they are talking about molecules, and sometimes they are talking about a certain volume of gas. For example, if there was one molecule of ozone in every million molecules found in a sample of the air, the concentration of ozone would be one part per million. If one gallon of ozone was found in every million gallons of air tested, the concentration would still be one part per million *by volume*, but because ozone molecules do not take up the same space that all the other gases do, there could be more or less than one molecule per million others in the sample. It is a hard thing to picture a million of anything, of course, and talking about the "space taken up" (or volume) of one invisible gas mixing with others is almost impossible to imagine. But scaling things down can help. Picture ninety-nine pennies lying on a desktop, with one dime mixed in among them. The "concentration" of dimes in that collection would be one dime per hundred. If you had a 999 pennies and one dime, it would be one dime per thousand, and so on. That is not too complicated.

It is a bit harder to imagine things by volume, but again, scaling things down should help. Imagine that you had ninety-nine cups of dimes on the table in front of you and one cup of quarters. If you were asked what the concentration of quarters was *in cups*, you would answer "one in one hundred." But if you were asked what the concentration of quarters was by number, you would realize that it is much less than one in one hundred, because many more dimes will fit into a cup than will quarters.

Carbon Dioxide

Carbon dioxide is a colorless and odorless gas. Each molecule of carbon dioxide is made up of one atom of carbon and two atoms of oxygen. Its chemical abbreviation, CO_2, reflects that proportion. Most of you know that carbon dioxide is the substance that plants take in from the air, converting it to sugar by tapping the power of sunlight, in the process called photosynthesis. That makes carbon dioxide essential for the growth of plants, trees, and crops. What you might not know is that carbon dioxide is also the gas that makes soda bubbly, as well as part of the gas that is released when you burn a piece of wood, coal, or gasoline.

Compared to nitrogen and oxygen, carbon dioxide only accounts for a small percentage of the atmosphere. In fact, only 386 parts out of every million parts of the atmosphere are made up of carbon dioxide. Despite that relative scarcity, researchers consider carbon dioxide a strong global warming gas. And they point out that carbon dioxide levels have increased by nearly 30 percent from the late eighteenth century to the present, and they are still rising.

Before the industrial revolution, when people started using large amounts of energy and causing significant changes to the environment by expanding farms and cities where forests used to be, carbon dioxide levels hovered near 280 parts per million, by volume. But even before humans were acting to change carbon dioxide levels, other forces did. Dips as low as 200 parts per million or surges into the mid-300 parts per million have been observed by climate investigators looking at air bubbles trapped in polar ice cores.

The carbon in carbon dioxide is an element present in many forms of solid, liquid, and gaseous materials on earth. In fact, carbon moves through a cycle on the earth, spewing out into the atmosphere from the core of the earth when volcanoes erupt, then being trapped by land and water plants as sugar (sugar is made mostly of carbon). When combined with minerals, that sugar is used to make all the other chemicals in the bodies of plants and animals. After water, carbon makes up the largest part of your body, as it does for all animals and plants. The carbon bound up in living tissues is eventually returned to the carbon cycle after the animals and plants die. Through rainfall and the action of rivers and streams, carbon eventually washes out into the oceans and sinks to the bottom. In some areas of the ocean, and even some areas on land, a phenomenon called "plate tectonics" causes some of the earth's surface layers to slowly return to the core of the earth, and much of the carbon that plants and animals take out of the atmosphere is pulled back with it. Eventually, after the residual animal and plant materials are converted back to pure carbon, it is paired up with two molecules of oxygen, and carbon dioxide is spewed back out of volcanoes, starting the cycle all over again.

While most of the carbon cycle is not altered by human action, some of it is. Carbon dioxide that is bound up in things like coal, oil, and wood can be released into the atmosphere much more quickly than it would through nonhuman processes. Human activities such as fuel burning and planting crops can change the carbon dioxide concentration of the atmosphere. So can changes in ocean currents, volcanic eruptions, changes in atmospheric humidity, and other things.

Because carbon dioxide stays in the atmosphere for a long time and can be put into the air faster than it is taken out by plants or other processes, carbon dioxide can build up in the atmosphere over time. The total amount of carbon moving through the atmosphere because of *direct* human activity is small in any given year—less than 5 percent of the total. But the carbon dioxide humans release into the air stays there for about 120 years, and over many years, even a small contribution can add up to a big impact.[1] Other human actions besides fuel use (such as turning forested land into farmland or urban development) can also have a significant impact on the carbon cycle because of human impacts on the storage of carbon in vegetation and soil.

Since highly accurate, direct measurement of carbon dioxide levels began only in 1957, most evidence of carbon dioxide's concentration in the past comes from indirect measurements, such as the analysis of gas bubbles trapped in Antarctic glaciers. Though this kind of indirect measurement is less accurate than directly measuring the carbon dioxide in the air, they are the only way we can determine what past levels of carbon dioxide were. That has helped scientists to understand how unusual the recent increases in carbon dioxide have been, from a historical point of view. But there are still many poorly understood parts of the carbon cycle. Scientists are still unsure about why the increase in carbon dioxide level sometimes comes

Changes in volcanic eruptions can cause changes in the concentration of carbon dioxide in the atmosphere. Shown are researchers on Mt. Saint Helens, which last erupted in 1980.

before global warming, but sometimes comes after. They are also unsure of how much carbon dioxide the plants of the world can absorb, and for how long.

Methane

Like carbon dioxide, methane is a colorless, odorless gas. One molecule of methane consists of one atom of carbon and four atoms of hydrogen, giving it a chemical name of CH_4. Methane is a major constituent of the "natural gas" that your stove, water heater, or other household devices use to heat water or to cook food.

Methane enters the atmosphere from a variety of sources, some of human origin, some of nonhuman origin. As a greenhouse gas, methane is a warming agent between five and fifty-six times more powerful than carbon dioxide. The reason this warming strength has such a broad range is because the warming strength of all the different greenhouse gases is compared to carbon dioxide, which has a very long lifetime in the atmosphere. In other words, once carbon dioxide is put into the air, it takes a long time for it to be removed from the air by plants or other natural forces. Methane, on the other hand, has a much shorter lifetime in the atmosphere, only about twelve years. If one compares the warming ability of one gallon of carbon dioxide versus one gallon of methane over a five-year period, the methane's greater ability to trap heat will be obvious and give it a much higher heat-trapping ability. But if one looks over twenty years, the methane originally released will have been taken out of the atmosphere, while most of the carbon dioxide will still be there, trapping heat.

Methane is considered a *trace gas*, because it is found at very low levels in the atmosphere—only 1.7 parts of methane are present in every million parts of air. But like carbon dioxide levels, methane levels have risen in the last hundred years. Methane's concentration in the atmosphere has increased nearly 150 percent since the beginning of the nineteenth century, with current levels being the highest ever recorded. Methane concentrations have recently leveled off since 1992, though climate investigators are unsure why.

Despite methane's low concentrations, some climate investigators have suggested that methane, more than carbon dioxide, has been the driving force behind rapid climate warmings in the distant past.[2] More recently, James Hansen, the same investigator who galvanized action with his 1988 testimony to Congress, has suggested that too much attention has been paid to carbon dioxide as a warming gas, when methane might be playing a more important role in recently observed global warming.[3]

Nitrous Oxide

Nitrous oxide is a colorless and almost odorless gas found in very low levels in the atmosphere. A molecule of nitrous oxide is made up of two atoms of nitrogen and one atom of oxygen. Nitrous oxide is also known by its nickname, "laughing gas," because it is sometimes used to make people feel relaxed and sleepy at the dentist's office, and, true to its name, it tends to make people a bit giggly. Nitrous oxide comes from a variety of sources, some of human origin, some of natural origin.

Nitrous oxide is a long-lived warming gas with a relative warming strength up to nearly 300 times that of carbon dioxide. Like methane, nitrous oxide has a shorter lifespan than carbon dioxide (114 years versus 120 for carbon dioxide). This means that nitrous oxide could have more or less global warming impact than carbon dioxide, depending on whether one is looking at shorter terms or longer terms.

Like methane, nitrous oxide is considered a trace gas in the atmosphere, but at still lower levels, around 0.3 parts per million of the atmosphere by volume. Nitrous oxide concentrations have increased in recent years. Before the industrial age, concentrations of nitrous oxide hovered at an average of 279 parts per billion by volume.

Ozone

Ozone is a slightly bluish, acrid-smelling gas composed of three atoms of oxygen bound together. You may be familiar with the smell of ozone—it is the tangy smell sometimes given off by electronic devices like your television set. Ozone plays many different roles in the environment, depending on where it is found, and several of those roles are linked to each other.

At the very top of the atmosphere, in the stratosphere, ozone is a beneficial gas. Up there, ozone stops certain harmful rays of the sun (called ultraviolet, or UV, rays) from penetrating down to the surface of the earth, where they could harm plants or animals. That ozone layer forms right where it is, when high-energy radiation from the sun breaks apart normal oxygen (made of two atoms of oxygen bound together), and all the free oxygen atoms can combine into groups of three. You have probably heard that there is a "hole" in that beneficial ozone layer, and there is. The hole in the stratospheric ozone layer is partly a natural process due to the way air circulates around the earth, and is partly a result of the actions of certain chemicals, called halocarbons. And this is where things get confusing. As will be discussed later, halocarbons are, themselves, global warming gases, but their effect on the stratospheric ozone layer is a separate process. Further complicating things, the ozone "hole" does change the way the earth's atmosphere retains heat. Finally, found down at ground level in a city, ozone is also called "smog," and can irritate people's eyes or the linings of their lungs.

Because of all those interactions, the impact of ozone on global warming can be downright confusing. At lower levels of the atmosphere (called the troposphere), scientists think that ozone exerts a warming force on the atmosphere. Tropospheric levels of ozone in the Northern Hemisphere may have doubled since the 1800s. But ozone concentrations in the Southern Hemisphere are uncertain, while at the Poles, tropospheric ozone concentrations seem to have fallen since the mid-1980s.

At higher, or stratospheric, altitudes, ozone exerts a cooling force upon the atmosphere. Stratospheric ozone also shields the earth from some of the sun's more dangerous types of radiation, including ultraviolet radiation, the kind that causes sunburn and skin cancer. Ozone concentrations in the stratosphere have been declining over much of the earth, as much as 2 percent each decade for the last thirty years.[4] Much

Sensors on balloons like this one yield information about the hole in the ozone layer.

of the decline in stratospheric ozone concentrations has been attributed to the destructive action of halocarbons, discussed below.

Aerosols

Aerosols are not gases but are liquid or solid particles small enough to stay suspended in the air, like fine mist. Both human and nonhuman processes generate aerosols. For example, when airplanes fly overhead, they leave a trail of aerosol droplets behind them, as the exhaust gases and unburned fuel go through chemical reactions with moisture in the air. When temperature and humidity conditions are right, this trail of aerosol droplets forms a brightly visible contrail behind the airplane.

Different aerosol types can have different impacts upon the climate. Some aerosol particles tend to reflect light or cause clouds to brighten, exerting a cooling effect on the atmosphere. Other aerosol particles tend to absorb light and can exert a warming effect. Aerosols do not remain in the atmosphere for long periods of time, tending to be washed out of the air by rainfall on a regular basis.

Most aerosols that humans create are believed to have a cooling effect on the climate. On a global basis, scientists think that this cooling effect could cancel out about 20 percent (and possibly more) of the predicted warming from all the other greenhouse gases combined. But as with the observed warming, the cooling effects of aerosols are local and depend on local aerosol types and concentrations.

The contrails behind these jets are made of aerosol droplets formed from exhaust gases and unburned fuel.

The exact way that aerosols act as cooling agents is poorly understood. Besides directly scattering incoming sunlight, particulate matter can also increase the brightness, formation, and lifetime of clouds, affecting the reflection of incoming solar radiation back to space.

The impact of aerosols on climate is still one of the most hotly debated issues among climate investigators. Some scientists argue that the cooling effects of aerosols have canceled out or hidden warming from other greenhouse gases. They say this will lead to more warming in the future, because different air pollution control laws are making aerosol concentrations decline. Other investigators argue that aerosols did not cause this kind of masking of global warming in the past. They observe that cooling and warming aerosols could cancel each other out altogether, and global warming theories simply overpredicted warming in the past. These investigators predict that there will be lower levels of global warming in the future, regardless of aerosol changes.

Halocarbons

Halocarbons are human-made chemicals that are used as cooling agents and propellants in a broad range of devices such as air conditioners and refrigerators. In the past, halocarbons were also used as a gas for puffing up styrofoam and for cleaning off electrical circuit boards.

There are many different types of halocarbons, some of which have been banned from production because of concerns about their adverse impacts upon the stratospheric ozone layer. Because of their destructive action on the stratospheric ozone layer, developed countries agreed not to produce certain halocarbons as part of an international accord called the Montreal Protocol. Other halocarbons that do not hurt the stratospheric ozone layer remain in production. Halocarbons are thought to be very powerful warming gases. Some kinds are over ten thousand times more capable of trapping heat than is carbon dioxide. Halocarbons can also be very long-lived, persisting for many hundreds of years in the atmosphere after release. One group, called the perfluorocarbons, are virtually "immortal," persisting for up to fifty thousand years. Offsetting their greater heat-trapping ability is the fact that halocarbons are found at much lower concentrations than the other greenhouse gases. Whereas carbon dioxide is measured in parts per million, and methane in parts per billion, halocarbons are measured in parts per trillion.

Halocarbons can exert a variety of impacts on the climate, depending on the type of halocarbon involved and where it is found. Current scientific understanding of the global warming impact of halocarbons suggests that the ozone-depleting halocarbons (the production of which has been banned in many countries) exert a cooling effect. The newer halocarbons, those that do not destroy high-altitude ozone, seem to be pure warming gases but with a considerably lower warming potential than the chemicals they replaced.

Because ozone chemistry in the atmosphere is so complex, scientists are uncertain about the ultimate impact of halocarbons on climate change.

6

Questionable Characters

Along with the extensive cast of characters discussed in the previous chapter, climate investigators are faced with some possible causes of global warming that are not well understood. Some of these potential climate change factors are positive—that is, they could cause greater warming; some are negative—that is, they could cause less global warming.

Water Vapor

Water vapor is the most abundant of the greenhouse gases and the dominant contributor to the natural greenhouse effect.

On average, about 0.4 percent of all the molecules in the air are water molecules. That is about ten times as common as carbon dioxide. But the amount of water in the air varies by location. Some areas can have as much as 2 percent of the air filled with water vapor. Glaciers and ice caps contain about 1,900 times as much water as the total atmosphere does, while ground and surface waters hold about 660 times as much water as the total atmosphere does. The oceans hold over 100,000 times as much water as the entire earth's atmosphere.

Besides the total amount of water vapor in the atmosphere, climate investigators have to consider its distribution at different altitudes and locations, because small changes in water vapor can have significant local effects on climate. Almost all water vapor enters the atmosphere by evaporation, and about 90 percent of the earth's water vapor is in the half of the atmosphere closest to the earth's surface. At typical United States temperatures, one to 2 percent of the air molecules near the surface are water vapor.

Water vapor plays many roles in influencing the climate, functioning as either a climate-warming force or a climate-cooling force. When it enters the atmosphere via evaporation, water vapor cools the surface from which it evaporates, and thus is a cooling force. The same thing happens to you when water evaporates from your skin—it cools you down. Another way that water vapor can cool the climate is when it takes the form of clouds that reflect incoming solar energy away from the earth.

Low-level clouds are thicker and tend to cool the earth by reflecting energy away. By contrast, water vapor in the form of thin cirrus clouds acts as a warming force because it lets incoming energy pass through but stops some of the energy from bouncing back out into space. Water vapor can also warm the climate because it traps heat even more effectively than carbon dioxide.

Most climate investigators think that a warmer world will lead to higher levels of water vapor and cause still more global warming. But Richard Lindzen, a respected climatologist at the Massachusetts Institute of Technology, thinks otherwise. Lindzen points out that even if added evaporation due to global warming does occur, the higher energy levels predicted for storms at that temperature would force the vapor back out of the air more quickly, possibly canceling out the potential amplifying effect on warming.

Further complicating the situation, climate investigators are not even sure if recently experienced warming has led to higher levels of water vapor in the air, as theories say it should.

Using satellites, some researchers have started gathering detailed information on water vapor levels in the atmosphere since the late 1970s. Some investigators have seen what appear to be slight increases in water vapor in various parts of the atmosphere, up to 13 percent. But other researchers, looking at the same information, have found just the opposite, pointing to an apparent drying of the atmosphere rather than increased moisture levels.

Because the information about water vapor levels is so limited, it is not possible to know which investigators are right at this time. And what little information investigators do have suffers from the same kind of problems discussed for other climate information. Changes in measuring systems, changes in instrument type, limited geographic coverage, limited time span, and many other factors make information on water vapor too sketchy to allow

Water vapor in the form of clouds can either warm or cool the earth, depending on the type of cloud and its distance from the earth's surface.

for strong conclusions about how it has reacted to recent global warming or how it is likely to affect future global warming.

A Changing Sun

Rather than burning with a steady output, the sun burns hotter and cooler over time. Several cycles of increased or decreased solar output have been identified, including cycles at intervals of eleven years, twenty-two years, and eighty-eight years.

Highly accurate satellite measurements of the sun's output have only been taken since the early 1980s. But investigators can also learn about the sun's output from ice cores and tree rings. One way they can do this is by looking at the impact of cosmic rays (a type of radiation from the sun), which produce unique radioactive versions of certain elements. Beryllium is one such element; when it is hit by cosmic rays, some of it is changed into a slightly radioactive form that gets incorporated into trees as they grow or gets trapped in bubbles in ice masses, just as carbon dioxide does.

Using this evidence, scientists have formed an idea of what the levels of solar energy reaching the earth have been. Taken as a whole, the evidence suggests that from 1600 A.D. to the present, the sun has clearly been running hotter, increasing the level of solar output, which constitutes the main natural influence on the temperature of the earth's climate system.

Some investigators suggest that this increased

solar energy level may have been responsible for half of the increase in temperature from 1900 through 1970 and for one third of the warming seen since 1970. Other climate investigators argue that the sun's output has not increased that much and think that it has not caused a significant share of the global warming observed since the 1970s.

Investigators use satellites to gather a wealth of information about climate, including temperature, water vapor levels, and solar output.

Natural Variability?

Still other investigators think that the recently observed global warming is not of human origin at all, but rather, is part of earth's natural cycle of climate change. These researchers point to past periods in earth's history, when average temperatures equaled or exceeded the temperatures seen today.

A long-standing assumption of many climate investigators is that recently observed warming is abnormal and thus is likely to be due to human activity. But other researchers point to evidence that temperatures in the past have shown more rapid and extreme climate change than the recent changes seen globally. In Greenland, temperatures increased in the past by as much as 7°C over only a few decades. Sea-surface temperatures in the Norwegian Sea also changed rapidly in the past, warming by as much as 5°C in less than forty years.[1] Recently, some climate investigators have suggested that these temperature fluctuations were not only local in scale, but were actually global. If past global average temperatures exceeded those of today, these investigators argue, it is possible that we are simply experiencing a normal fluctuation, and while human activity may be slightly accentuating that fluctuation, it is not the cause.

7

So Whodunnit?

With all this mass of climate information, it is hard to see what is really going on. The evidence is mixed, it is often of poor quality, and sometimes it is outright contradictory.

One of the ways that climate researchers go beyond the physical evidence, even the circumstantial evidence, is with the use of computerized models of the earth's climate. You might not know it, but you are probably familiar with some computer models already. Every time you play a video game, you are using a computer model. Computer models are one way of testing theories of global warming. Evidence is fed into the models, and the models calculate whether or not something has really changed, and if so, what is responsible for the change.

Computer models work by assigning mathematical equations to things that happen in the real world. In climate models, investigators assign equations to things such as the incoming heat from the sun, the outgoing heat from the clouds or surface, the heat moved around in the ocean, the heat moved around in the air, and so on. Then they link all those equations together, and they do experiments with this model to see what might happen if they changed one part or another.

Computer models have been used to ask three main questions in global warming research. The first question is, "Is the climate changing abnormally?" This is sometimes called the *detection* of climate change. The second question that computer models are used to explore is, "What is causing the climate change we have observed?" This is sometimes called the *attribution* of climate change. Finally, computer models are used to explore the question, "What would happen if the earth got warmer?" This is sometimes called the *impact* of climate change. The models can show how changes in the climate might affect humans, plants, and society. Answering each of these questions involves using different types of models that reflect different elements of climate science.

In trying to detect whether the climate is changing

If you have played a video or computer game, you have used a computer model. Scientists use computer models to test theories of global warming.

abnormally, investigators are trying to find out whether the warming that has been observed is greater than random chance. Computer models have been run with all of the evidence discussed previously, and more as well, looking back over a thousand years to determine whether or not recent changes in the climate are from natural variation or not. With the power of new computer models, IPCC investigators are increasingly convinced that "most of the observed warming over the last 50 years is likely to have been due to the increase in greenhouse gas concentrations."[1] In looking for the cause of climate change, climate investigators for the IPCC and elsewhere are also increasingly confident that Arrhenius, Fourier, and Hansen were right—greenhouse gases seem to be causing a slight heating of the earth, at least over the last fifty years.

But when it comes to making predictions of the future, climate investigators might as well consult a fortune-teller. Computer models used to make predictions of the future are much less advanced than those used to detect global warming or to examine potential causes. While some investigators in the IPCC place confidence in long-term and regional predictions of increased temperature, sea level, rainfall, and so on, others are much less sure about predictive climate models.

Still, computer models are the only tools that climate investigators have to ask the most important questions about climate change. Is the climate changing abnormally? If so, what is behind the change, and what will the future look like? While

Greenhouse gases are believed to trap heat around the earth much in the same way that the glass walls of a greenhouse trap heat inside.

the computer models strongly suggest that it has warmed up a bit, and that some of that warming has been caused by human emission of greenhouse gases, the verdict will not be in for some time. Questions about which human activity is causing recent warming, and what things might look like in a warmer world, will take some years to answer, while climate investigators continue to dig for more information.

8

What Can
Be Done?

While there are many arguments among climate investigators over whether humanity is changing the climate, there are still more arguments about what should be done. Some people argue that we know enough about the climate to take actions that would reduce humanity's emissions of greenhouse gases, heading most of the problems off at the pass. Others argue that humanity does not have to reduce its greenhouse gas emissions, but can plant more trees in order to pull excess carbon dioxide out of the air. Still others argue that the uncertainties about how the climate works, and about humanity's role in changing it, limit our ability to act intelligently. They argue for more research or for actions that will benefit humanity and the environment immediately but will also reduce humanity's production of greenhouse gases in case climate change turns out to be a real problem.

Head 'Em Off at the Pass?

Some people favor a head-'em-off-at-the-pass approach to climate change. That is, being fairly sure that global warming is being sped up by human emission of certain greenhouse gases, they argue for laws that would make people reduce the amount of greenhouse gases emitted into the atmosphere. The Kyoto accord, a treaty proposed by the United Nations in 1997, is an example of that approach.

Supporters of this approach argue that rapid action to reduce greenhouse gas emissions can prevent a lot of the predicted climate changes that IPCC investigators have suggested lie in humanity's future. But others argue that this approach is premature. They point out that until we are really sure what is causing the global warming we have seen in recent years, passing laws to reduce greenhouse gas emissions is an arbitrary action that might not do any good. Furthermore, since the main way to reduce greenhouse gas emissions is to reduce the use of fossil fuels, this approach could be very expensive and leave society less able to deal with whatever climate changes might occur if we have picked the wrong target.

Lock Up the Carbon?

Other people think that instead of reducing the emission of greenhouse gases, we should take actions that pull carbon dioxide, the main greenhouse gas, back out of the air. They point out that plants naturally pull carbon dioxide out of the air, and, they observe, carbon dioxide can be kept from influencing the climate by keeping it locked up in solid form in trees, plants, and in woody material in the soil.

There are three major ways people propose to hold carbon dioxide in solid form and eliminate its global warming impacts. The first way involves forests. Sometimes, in different parts of the world, when trees are cut down for use as fuel, or for the paper or lumber industries, the area where the trees were is not replanted, or the land is put to non-forestry or nonfarming uses. Climate investigators looking for ways to pull carbon dioxide out of the air point out that this practice limits the earth's natural ability to regulate greenhouse gases, including carbon dioxide. Preventing this kind of long-term removal of plants or crops from areas that have had trees removed can increase the amount of carbon dioxide pulled out of the air.

Another approach to pulling carbon dioxide out of the air is to plant more trees, something almost everyone can support. Not only could more trees be planted in tree farms, but tree-planting can be increased in cities and on land that was farmed for a while but is no longer good for growing crops.

Besides using trees to remove carbon dioxide

from the air, some researchers think that a lot of carbon dioxide could also be stored in farm soils. They point out that some farming practices could help keep carbon dioxide locked away in the soil, rather than putting it back into the air where it might warm the climate. Tilling the soil (digging it up prior

Some experts advocate tree planting as a measure to pull carbon out of the air.

to planting crops) is one farming practice that can put carbon dioxide back into the air, even though it is not always necessary for crop cultivation.

Also, changing the way that fertilizers and weed-killers are used can help keep more carbon-bearing matter underground and prevent it from being broken down by microbes living in the soil. Finally, farm fields that are left bare after harvest are more likely to release their soil carbon back into the atmosphere. Planting cover crops, such as beans, on areas that are not being used for other food crops can preserve soil nutrients and keep carbon dioxide locked up in the soil.[1]

More Investigation

One thing that virtually every climate investigator agrees on is that more research is badly needed. While the climate seems to have warmed recently, scientists need to find out whether the observed warming is a reflection of natural variability. While investigators are fairly sure that human action has caused some of the recently observed warming, it is still uncertain just how much of a role that action has played and how much it will play in future warming.

And while predictions of future warming and climate change suggest many dangers loom ahead, more research is needed to know how much that future climate might warm and how that warming might lead to more of the wacky weather that triggered the latest investigation back in 1988.

Chapter Notes

Chapter 1. The Debate Over Global Warming

1. "Statement of Dierdre A. Lee, Acting Deputy Director for Management, Office of Management and Budget Before the U.S. House of Representatives Subcommittee on National Economic Growth, Natural Resources, and Regulatory Affairs Committee on Government Reform and Oversight, and the United States Senate Subcommittee on Energy Research, Development, Production and Regulation, Committee on Energy and Natural Resources," May 20, 1999, <http://www.whitehouse.gov/omb/legislative/testimony/test052099ddm.html> (December 7, 2001).

2. James West, "1988 Midwest Drought," *USA Today*, November 21, 1999, <http://www.usatoday.com/2000/century/weather/stories/w88drought.htm> (December 7, 2001).

3. Gale E. Christianson, *Greenhouse: The 200-Year Story of Global Warming* (New York: Walker and Company, 1999), p. 197.

4. West.

5. Michigan Department of State Police, "Extreme Temperatures," n.d., <http://www.msp.state.mi.us/division/emd/Hazann2000/4-temperatures_MIHAZAN5.pdf> (December 10, 2001).

6. Kevin Sanders, "Yellowstone National Parks Year of Fire: The Great Fires of 1988," 1996,

<http://www.yellowstone-bearman.com/bearman/yfire.html> (December 7, 2001).

7. G. Jendritsky, WOM/UNESCO Sub-Forum on Science and Technology: Extreme Temperatures, Presentation, n.d., <http://www.unisdr.org/unisdr/forum/tempwmo.htm> (December 10, 2001).

8. James Hansen, "Testimony before the Committee on Energy and Commerce, United States House of Representatives," July 7, 1988.

9. Intergovernmental Panel on Climate Change (IPCC), *Climate Change 2001: The Scientific Basis* (Cambridge, Mass.: Cambridge University Press, 2001.

Chapter 2. What Is This Theory of Global Warming?

1. N. Murray and M. Holman, "The Role of Chaotic Resonances in the Solar System," *Nature*, vol. 410, April 12, 2001, pp. 773–779.

2. Adapted from A. Bernarde, *Global Warning ... Global Warming* (New York: John Wiley & Sons, 1992), p. 26.

3. James Rodger Fleming, *Historical Perspectives on Climate Change* (New York: Oxford University Press, 1998), p 58.

4. Ibid.

5. Ibid.

6. Ibid.

7. Barbara J. Finlayson-Pitts and James N. Pitts, Jr., *Chemistry of the Upper and Lower Atmosphere* (New York: Academic Press, 2000), p. 762.

8. Fleming, p 58.

9. Intergovernmental Panel on Climate Change (IPCC), *Climate Change 2001, Impacts, Adaptations*

and Vulnerability (Cambridge, Mass.: Cambridge University Press, 2001), p. 12.

10. Richard Stone, "If the Mercury Soars, So May Health Hazards," News and Comment, *Science*, vol. 267, February 17, 1995, pp. 957–958; Rita R. Colwell, "Global Climate and Infectious Disease: The Cholera Paradigm," Association Affairs, *Science*, vol. 274, December 20, 1996, pp. 2025–2031; Gary Taubes, "Apocalypse Not," News and Comment, *Science*, vol. 278, November 7, 1997, pp. 1004–1006.

Chapter 3. Hard Evidence of Global Warming

1. The largest collection of surface temperature data is maintained by the United States National Oceanographic and Atmospheric Association, <www.noaa.gov> (December 7, 2001).

2. Adapted from D.E. Parker, P. D. Jones, A. Bevan and C.K. Folland, "Interdecadal changes of surface temperature since the late 19th century," *Journal of Geophysical Research*, vol. 99, 1994, pp. 14373–14399 (and updates).

3. Patrick J. Michaels and Robert C. Balling, Jr., *The Satanic Gases: Clearing the Air About Global Warming* (Washington, D.C.: Cato Institute, 2000), pp. 75–91.

4. Kenneth Green, *Exploring the Science of Climate Change* (Los Angeles: Reason Public Policy Institute, 1997), p. 19.

5. James Rodger Fleming, *Historical Perspectives on Climate Change* (New York: Oxford University Press, 1998), pp. 17–18; Michael L. Parsons, *Global Warming, the Truth Behind the Myth* (New York: Plenum Press, 1995), p. 127.

6. S.A. Changnon, "A rare long record of deep soil temperatures defines temporal temperature changes and an urban heat island," *Climatic Change*, vol. 42, July 1999, pp. 531–538.

7. Ibid.

8. Adapted from "Heat Island Reduction Initiative," *U.S. Environmental Protection Agency Global Warming Page*, n.d., <http://www.epa.gov/globalwarming/actions/local/heatisland/> (April 18, 2002).

9. John Christy, written testimony before the United States Senate Committee on Environment and Public Works, May 2, 2001.

10. Adapted from Parker, Jones, Bevan, and Folland.

11. J.R. Christy, R.W. Spencer, and W.D. Brasell, "MSU Tropospheric temperatures: Data set construction and radiosonde comparisons," *Journal of Atmospheric and Oceanic Technology*, vol. 17, 2000, pp. 1153–1170 (and updates).

12. J.K. Angell, "Variations and trends in tropospheric and stratospheric global temperature, 19582/8/0287," *Journal of Climate*, vol. 1, 1988, pp. 1296–1313 (and updates).

13. National Research Council, *Reconciling Observations of Global Temperature Change* (Washington, D.C.: National Academy Press, 2000), p. 2.

14. J. R. Petit et al., "Climate and atmospheric history of the past 420,000 years from the Vostok ice core, Antarctica," *Nature*, vol. 393, June 3, 1999, pp. 429–436.

15. Paleoclimatology Program, United States National Oceanographic and Aeronautic

Administration (NOAA), <http://www.ngdc.noaa. gov/paleo/borehole/core.html> (December 7, 2001).

16. J. Jouzel et al., "Validity of the temperature reconstruction from water isotopes in ice cores," *Journal of Geophysical Research*, vol. 102, no. C12, November 30, 1997, pp. 471–487.

17. Bernhard Stauffer, "Cornucopia of ice core results," *Nature*, vol. 399, June 3, 1999, pp. 412–413.

18. Gordon Jacoby, Roseanne D'Arrigo, and Gregory Wiles, "Tree Rings to Extend North Pacific Climate Records Over Recent Centuries," n.d., *NOAA Climate and Global Change Program Page*, <www.ncdc.noaa.gov/ogp/papers/jacoby.html> (March 7, 2002).

19. Edward R. Cook, "Temperature Histories from Tree Rings and Corals," *Climate Dynamics*, vol. 11, 1995, pp. 211–222.

Chapter 4. Circumstantial Evidence of Global Warming

1. Intergovernmental Panel on Climate Change (IPCC), *Climate Change 1995: The Science of Climate Change* (Cambridge, Mass.: Cambridge University Press, 1996), p. 142.

2. Intergovernmental Panel on Climate Change (IPCC), *Climate Change 2001: The Scientific Basis* (Cambridge, Mass.: Cambridge University Press, 2001), p. 641.

3. Ibid., p. 666.

4. Ibid., p. 641.

5. Intergovernmental Panel on Climate Change (IPCC), *Climate Change 1995: The Science of Climate Change*, p. 158.

6. Intergovernmental Panel on Climate Change (IPCC), *Climate Change 2001: The Scientific Basis*, p. 123.

7. Ibid., p. 124.

8. Ibid., p. 129.

9. Intergovernmental Panel on Climate Change (IPCC), *Climate Change 1995: The Science of Climate Change*, pp. 650–654.

10. Intergovernmental Panel on Climate Change (IPCC), *Climate Change 2001: The Scientific Basis*, p. 30.

11. Ibid., p. 5.

12. Intergovernmental Panel on Climate Change (IPCC), *Climate Change 1995: The Science of Climate Change*, p. 173.

13. Michael L. Parsons, *Global Warming: The Truth Behind the Myth* (New York: Plenum Press, 1995), pp. 112–117.

Chapter 5. The Primary Suspects— Greenhouse Gases

1. For an up-to-date listing of the concentrations, lifetimes, and global warming ability of the different greenhouse gases, visit the Carbon Dioxide Information Analysis Center, hosted by the Oak Ridge National Laboratories, <http://cdiac.esd.ornl.gov/pns/current_ghg.html> (December 7, 2001).

2. Richard A. Kerr, "A smoking gun for an ancient methane discharge," *Science*, vol. 286, November 19, 1999, p. 1465.

3. James Hansen et al., "Climate Forcings in the Industrial Era," *Proceedings of the National*

Academy of Sciences, vol. 95, October 1998, pp. 12753–12758.

4. Intergovernmental Panel on Climate Change (IPCC), *Climate Change 2001: The Scientific Basis* (Cambridge, Mass.: Cambridge University Press, 2001), p. 256.

Chapter 6. Questionable Characters

1. M. E. Raymo et al., "Millennial-scale climate instability during the early Pleistocene epoch," *Nature*, vol. 392, April 16, 1998, pp. 669–702.

Chapter 7. So Whodunnit?

1. Intergovernmental Panel on Climate Change (IPCC), *Climate Change 2001: The Scientific Basis* (Cambridge, Mass.: Cambridge University Press, 2001), p. 10.

Chapter 8. What Can Be Done?

1. Steven Schroeder and Kenneth Green, *Reducing Global Warming Through Forestry and Agriculture* (Los Angeles: Reason Public Policy Institute, 2001), p. 4.

Glossary

aerosol—Microscopic droplets of water and other chemicals that can either trap heat like a greenhouse gas or reflect heat away from the earth.

atmosphere—The layer of gases that surrounds a planet.

carbon dioxide—A greenhouse gas consisting of one atom of carbon and two of oxygen, abbreviated CO_2.

chaos—The tendency of complex systems to vary randomly over time.

climate—The long-term (thirty-year) average pattern of the weather.

ecosystem—An assembly of plants, animals, insects, and other living things that constitute a defined ecological system. Examples include forests, deserts, and wetlands.

evaporation—When water passes from a liquid into a vapor.

fossil fuels—Fuels derived from the tissues of living things from long ago. Fossil fuels include coal, peat, oil, and natural gas.

global warming—Warming of the earth's surface through the heat-trapping effects of certain greenhouse gases in the atmosphere.

greenhouse effect—The trapping of heat by certain greenhouse gases in the atmosphere.

greenhouse gas—Any gas that can trap heat in a planet's atmosphere that would otherwise pass back out into space.

halocarbons—Chemicals used in refrigerators and air conditioners. Halocarbons are strong greenhouse gases but are found at very low concentrations in the atmosphere.

home-range—The normal living area of a plant, animal, or insect.

invertebrates—Animals without a backbone, such as insects, octopuses, snails, clams, etc.

IPCC (Intergovernmental Panel on Climate Change)—A group of scientists gathered together by the United Nations to write about climate change science, impacts, and policy approaches.

latitude—A measure of distance north or south of the earth's equator.

longitude—A measure of distance east or west from an imaginary line running from the North to South Poles, passing through the city of Greenwich, England.

methane—A greenhouse gas consisting of one atom of carbon and four of hydrogen, abbreviated CH_4.

nitrous oxide—A greenhouse gas consisting of one atom of nitrogen and two atoms of oxygen. Also known as laughing gas.

ozone—A greenhouse gas consisting of three atoms of oxygen. Ozone plays many roles in the environment and is found at different levels of the atmosphere. In some cases, ozone can be protective, in other cases, it can cause harm to human, plant, and animal health directly.

rain gauge—A device for measuring rainfall.

smog—Another name for ozone when it is close to the ground, where people can inhale it.

soot—Fine particles of matter created through the combustion of fuel or mechanical friction.

stratosphere—The part of the atmosphere above the troposphere, extending about twenty miles above the earth's surface.

thermostat—A device that controls heating and cooling systems to maintain a specified temperature in an enclosed space, such as a room or refrigerator.

Third Assessment Report—The most recent report of the Intergovernmental Panel on Climate Change, released in July 2001.

troposphere—The lower part of the atmosphere, from ground level up, ranging from 4 to 11 miles above the ground depending on where one is located on the earth's surface.

Tyndall Effect—The scattering of light by dust and large molecules. This is the effect that makes the sky look blue. Named for the discoverer, John Tyndall.

wetlands—Areas where there is a frequent and prolonged presence of water at or near the soil surface. Swamps, marshes, and bogs are examples of wetlands.

For More Information

Center for the Study of Carbon Dioxide and Global Change
P.O. Box 25697
Tempe, Ariz. 85285-5697
(480) 966-3719

Reason Public Policy Institute
3415 S. Sepulveda Blvd., Suite 400
Los Angeles, Calif. 90034
(310) 391-2245

United Nations Intergovernmental Panel on Climate Change
c/o World Meteorological Organization
7 bis Avenue de la Paix
CP 2300
CH 1211 Geneva 2, Switzerland

United States Environmental Protection Agency
Ariel Rios Building
1200 Pennsylvania Avenue, N.W.
Washington, D.C. 20460
(202) 260-2090

Further Reading

Edmonds, Alex. *Greenhouse Effect*. Brookfield, Conn.: Millbrook Press, 1997.

Pringle, Laurence P. *Global Warming: The Threat of Earth's Changing Climate*. New York: SeaStar Books, 2001.

Roleff, Tamara L., Scott Barbour, and Karin L. Swisher. *Global Warming: Opposing Viewpoints*. Farmington Hills, Mich.: Greenhaven Press, 1997.

Stein, Paul. *Global Warming: A Threat to Our Future*. New York: Rosen Publishing, 2001.

Tesar, Jenny E. *Global Warming*. Bridgewater, N.J.: Replica Books, 1991.

Internet Addresses

NOAA Paleoclimatology Program
<http://www.ngdc.noaa.gov/paleo/paleo.html>

United States Environmental Protection Agency Global Warming Kids Page
<http://www.epa.gov/globalwarming/kids/>

USA Today Weather, Understanding Climate
<http://www.usatoday.com/weather/wclimat0.htm>

Index